D0886863

ICE CREAM

Edible

Series Editor: Andrew F. Smith

EDIBLE is a revolutionary new series of books dedicated to food and drink that explores the rich history of cuisine. Each book reveals the global history and culture of one type of food or beverage.

Already published

Ice Cream

A Global History

Laura B. Weiss

REAKTION BOOKS

To my father, Edmund Simonds,
whose love of ice cream inspired this book.

Published by Reaktion Books Ltd
33 Great Sutton Street
London EC1V 0DX, UK
www.reaktionbooks.co.uk

First published 2011

Printed and bound in China by C&C Offset Printing Co. Ltd

British Library Cataloguing in Publication Data

Weiss, Laura.
Ice cream: a global history. – (Edible)
1. Ice cream, ices, etc – History
I. Title II. Series
641.8´62-DC22

ISBN 978 1 86189 979 2

Contents

Introduction:
Everyone Loves Ice Cream

I scream, you scream,
we all scream for ice cream!
Howard Johnson, Billy Moll and Robert King, 1927

It's called *gelato* in Italy, *glace* in France and *morozhenoe* in Russia. From Tokyo to Turin, from Denver to Delhi, everyone loves ice cream. With the possible exception of romance – 'Your love is better than ice cream', singer Sarah McLachlan has crooned – there are few of life's pleasures, culinary or otherwise, that can match ice cream's potent allure.

What accounts for the sweet frozen treat's irresistible appeal?

First, ice cream is just plain delectable. Composed of cream or milk, sweeteners and flavourings, which are churned and frozen, ice cream boasts an icy sumptuousness. What's more, ice cream packs an emotional wallop. Stoking the pleasure-producing regions of the brain, ice cream is known for its ability to generate feelings of well-being, 'It's amazing how quickly you recover from misery when someone offers you ice cream', marvelled teenager Eugene Jerome in *Brighton Beach Memoirs*, American playwright Neil Simon's coming-of-age play.

Of course, ice cream tantalizes the taste buds and delights the eye. There's the frothy ice cream soda sipped through a straw at the neighbourhood soda fountain. There's the luxurious taste of a gelato-topped cone, relished while strolling through the streets of Rome. There are the Indian *kulfiwalas* hawking cardamom-perfumed kulfi on the streets of Delhi and Mumbai. There's melting hot fudge enrobing a scoop of vanilla ice cream in a decadent pairing of heat and cold that rarely fails to thrill children and adults alike.

But ice cream also conjures up powerful memories – sounds recalled from childhood or distinctive events, such as birthdays or patriotic celebrations. One of the measures of ice cream's potent appeal is how the mere sight of the sweet, frozen confection immediately taps into memories of carefree childhood idylls, not to mention the innocence of simpler times. There's the merry call of the ice cream man – trolling city streets in a boxy white truck in New York or on a bicycle in Saigon – and his promise of carefree summer days. (My own earliest ice cream memories are bittersweet. Hobbled by a dairy allergy, it was only at age four that I finally got to sample the frozen dessert. It was vanilla – and it was simply the most heavenly food I had ever tasted.)

As befits a food so strongly identified with fun, the story of ice cream is a lively one. It's a moveable feast peppered with Chinese emperors and English kings, former slaves, women inventors, shrewd businessmen, Italian immigrant hokey pokey ice cream vendors, a gourmand First Lady, health food advocates, temperance apostles and modern-day food snobs.

Ice cream – at various points in its history, it's been called 'ices', 'iced-cream' and 'cream' – began its ascent to worldwide dessert fame as a luxury food that only the upper crust could afford. As ice cream travelled through history, it

Ice cream offers a brief respite for children in war-torn Iraq.

evolved from a food identified with an opulent lifestyle into a mainstream consumer sensation coveted by paupers and princes alike.

Though the Chinese are said to have been the first to fashion a dairy-like frozen dessert, ice cream as we now know it was initially formulated in Europe, principally in Italy, but also in France, England and other parts of the Continent. Ice cream then travelled across the Atlantic to America. In fact, Americans like to claim ice cream as their national dessert, conferring upon it a status rivalling the mythic apple pie. It's true that American entrepreneurs and culinary inventors did contribute mightily to ice cream's meteoric rise on to the world food stage. Worldwide favourites like the cone, the sundae and the soda were either created or popularized in the US. What's more, the soda fountain is an American icon, and the commercial ice cream industry was also spawned and nurtured by US business and culinary talent. In fact, many of today's most recognized global ice cream brands, such as Häagen-Dazs and Baskin-Robbins, claim American roots.

Yet without culinary influences from the Old World, ice cream in the US would never have evolved into the global mass-market phenomenon it eventually became. Early Italian, French and English confectioners created ice cream recipes and techniques that spawned the modern ice cream that we cherish today. Italian immigrants spread the art of ice cream making throughout Europe and North America. There, they sold their wares on the streets of New York, London, Berlin and other cities, where they paved the way for ice cream to emerge as one of the world's most beloved street foods.

Despite the sizeable American influence, indigenous ice cream cultures flourish worldwide. For example, Italian gelato is prized by ice cream connoisseurs everywhere. In Turkey and parts of the Middle East, *salepi dondurma*, an ice cream enhanced with orchid root, continues to flourish.

Still today, national ice cream traditions are fading, blending into a universal version of what once was a distinctive local dessert. In fact, ice cream has been transformed into a culinary blank slate which can take on the colouration of just about any food culture. A Long Island, New York ice cream maker produces kulfi – using a pre-mixed American ice cream base. In Brooklyn, a group of women express their Eastern European Jewish culinary roots through ice cream. Matzoh Crunch, anyone?

Even gelato, that supposedly sacrosanct Italian ice cream, has been transformed (corrupted, some might say) by outside influences. There's now green tea and cheddar cheese gelato being served from Des Moines to Delhi. In Italy, I sampled flavours like ginger and spicy Aztec chocolate, some clearly not handmade and displaying flavour notes culled from regions far beyond Florence and Rome. In fact some might ask at this point: is gelato even Italian any more?

Ice cream also evolved into a celebrated cultural icon, appearing in artistic works as varied as Picasso paintings and Hollywood movies. Who can forget George Bailey in the 1946 Frank Capra classic *It's a Wonderful Life*, dishing up chocolate ice cream to Mary at the local ice cream fountain – while the young girl whispers, 'George Bailey, I'll love you till the day I die'?

Over the years, historians have sometimes elected to focus on the myths and legends – not to mention the legendary disputes – that colour ice cream's trajectory through history. Did Catherine de Medici really bring ice cream to France? Who was the true creator of the ice cream sundae? These are some of the questions that culinary historians and ice cream lovers have pondered for decades.

Ice Cream will review some of these epic debates. But *Ice Cream* will focus even more on the story of how the frozen dessert was altered from a food for the high-born into the widely consumed mass-market product it has become today. Along the way, Old World and New World economic, social and culinary influences combined to create the sweet indulgence that few can manage to resist.

I

The Early Ice Cream Age

Ice cream is exquisite. What a pity it isn't illegal.

Voltaire

The history of ice cream begins, not with the familiar concoction of cream, sugar, eggs and flavouring, but with chilled non-dairy drinks. Iced drinks date back at least to the ancient Greeks and Romans. It is said that Emperor Nero enjoyed icy refreshments flavoured with wine or honey. But to prepare chilled drinks, it was necessary to secure a source of ice and keep it frozen for months at a time. In the centuries before mechanical refrigeration, the only way to accomplish this was to send labourers up nearby mountains to gather snow or ice and then store it in a place where it wouldn't melt. Mesopotamia is said to have contained ice houses 4,000 years ago. The Greeks and Romans brought snow and ice down from nearby peaks and stashed it in ice pits. Ice harvesting and storage to preserve food began in China around 1100 BC. And Alexander the Great, when he conquered Petra in 837, is said to have had pits dug and filled with snow.

In Japan, the fourth-century emperor Nintoku was so taken with ice and its ability to preserve food that he declared 1 June to be national ice day. One day, one of the imperial princes spotted an ice pit and asked how the ice was stored. He was told by a local peasant:

> The ground is excavated to a depth of over ten feet. The top is then covered with a roof of thatch. A thick layer of reed-grass is then spread, upon which the ice is laid. The months of summer have passed and yet it is not melted. As to its use – when the hot months come it is placed in water or *sake* and thus used.[1]

The prince carried the news of this amazing phenomenon back to his father, Nintoku, who promptly adopted the newfangled ice storage method.

It was the emperors of the Tang Dynasty (618–907 AD) who many historians believe were the first to feast on a frozen milk-like confection. Did this mixture resemble the ice cream of today? Hardly. Composed of cow, goat or buffalo milk that was fermented and heated with flour and camphor for flavouring and texture, this ancient frozen sweet was enhanced with exotic ingredients like dragon brain fragments and eyeballs. Camphor, culinary historian Elizabeth David has pointed out, lent texture and visual appeal to the concoction by making it flake like snow.[2] What's more, camphor was said to possess medicinal value – a benefit that would be ascribed to ice cream by cooks and inventors for centuries to come. Freezing the blend was achieved by enclosing it in metal tubes, then lowering these into an ice pool – much like today's Indian kulfi, which is placed in metal containers that are then submerged in ice.

What about that other 'China Connection', the oft-told tale that Marco Polo (1254–1324) brought ice cream to Europe from the Far East? Though it's a charming story, this durable yarn has been thoroughly debunked over the years.

David explained the source of the tale by conjecturing that Marco Polo may have happened upon *kumiss*, a fermented mare's milk found in Mongolia.[3] Other historians concede that the Venetian explorer may have tasted ices in China. But Polo almost certainly didn't bring recipes or information about freezing techniques back with him to Italy. Otherwise, why did it take the Italians three more centuries to begin experimenting with freezing methods?[4] And there are still other scholars who insist that Marco Polo couldn't possibly have brought ice cream back to Europe. The reason? The explorer, they say, probably never even made it as far as that exotic land.

Italy: The Birth of Ices and Ice Cream

Another ice cream myth with remarkable staying power is the story of how Catherine de Medici, as the fourteen-year-old bride of Henry, Duke of Orléans (and future King Henry II), introduced ices to the French when she moved north to marry him in 1533. There is absolutely no evidence to support this tale, which artfully infuses culinary history with a dash of romance.

How, then, did ice cream as we now know it evolve into today's much-prized dessert?

Since medieval times, Arabs had drunk a liquid refreshment called sherbet, or *sharab* or *sharabt* in Arabic. The Persians and the Turks both imbibed the refreshing drinks, which were flavoured with fruits like cherries, pomegranates or quinces.

Perhaps arriving in Europe with travellers who brought them back from the Middle East, frozen drinks soon became all the rage among the European aristocracy. Culinary historians Alberto Capatti and Massimo Montanari have written that Italians were the undisputed masters of the technique.[5] So influential were these Italian drinks that the French, for example, were taking notice. The Frenchman and confectioner Nicolas Audiger in *La maison reglée* (1692) advised his readers that 'the Italian style' was *the* prescribed method for creating chilled and frozen liquid refreshments.

Typically, the iced drinks were laced with wine, spices or fruits, such as peach and raspberry, to which sugar and water had been added. And in a foretaste of the health issues that would plague ice cream at various points in its history, some doctors declared chilled drinks a menace. Medical experts decried the public's fondness for the drinks, warning people that very cold foods could trigger a variety of dangerous maladies, such as paralysis. Yet Italians continued to consume ices, presumably spurning their doctors' advice in much the same way that many of today's ice cream lovers disregard warnings about the danger to their arteries of consuming fatty food.

By the middle of the seventeenth century iced drinks were being reworked into a frozen dessert made from sugar, flavourings such as strawberries or lemons, and ice or snow. These frozen confections, called *sorbetto*, seem to have developed first in Italy. It's possible, say historians, that Giambattista della Porta, who in 1559 described the process of freezing wine in glasses, was the father of frozen ices. By 1685, the poet, scientist, medical doctor and linguist Francesco Redi had written of the pleasures of ices in his poem *Arianna inferma*.[6] But it was Antonio Latini, an overseer of kitchen and food operations for a Spanish Viceroy in Naples, who is considered to have been the first person actually to write down recipes for making and serving *sorbetto* in Italian. In his account of 1692–4, *Lo scalco alla moderna*, or *The Modern Steward*, Latini described Naples as a hotbed of *sorbetto* production, which was not confined exclusively to the households of the aristocracy. Neapolitans, said Latini, were already committed makers and consumers of *sorbetto*. While it's tempting to imagine seventeenth-century *nonnas* whipping up batches of flavourful *sorbetto*, it's impossible to know how widespread the practice of making the frozen confection really was. Could you stroll down any back street in Naples and watch *sorbetto* being made? We'll never know. But regardless of whether the practice was commonplace, Latini clearly believed that there was room for improvement when it came to Neapolitans' frozen dessert-making technique.

When it came to flavours, Latini outlined a dazzling array of possibilities. He flavoured his ices with lemon, strawberry and chocolate, the last a relatively new ingredient which the Spanish conquistadors had brought back from Mexico and Central America in the late sixteenth century. Even more exotic flavourings ranged from pine cones to aubergine (eggplant). Interestingly, Latini also created a recipe for a milk sorbet. Laced with candied citron or pumpkin, the cooked mixture featured a carafe and a half of milk, as well as water and sugar. The entire concoction was then cooked before being submerged in the freezing mixture of snow and salt.

Most culinary historians dub Latini's milk sorbet 'the first ice cream'. Though freezing sweetened dairy preparations was new, sweetened cooked creams, the base for the new frozen dessert, were already a kitchen staple. Since the Middle Ages, European cooks had been regularly producing custards and creams. Spaniards made *crema Catalana* and Italians ate *crema della mia nonna* (my grandmother's cream). But it wouldn't have taken much culinary wizardry to transform early creams into ice cream. In fact, custard preparation was so commonplace that some early ice cream recipes didn't even bother to review how to make these egg- and milk-based mixtures.

Café Culture

Twenty years before Latini published his compilation of sorbet recipes, Frenchman Nicolas Lemery created the first recipes in French for flavoured ices in the 1674 volume *Recueil de curiositéz rares et nouvelles de plus admirables effets de la nature*. Lemery's collection was also published two decades later in English, as *Modern Curiosities of Art and Nature*.

But it was with the creation of a new drinking and dining institution that the French made perhaps their greatest contribution to the world's future enjoyment of ice cream. In 1686 a Sicilian, Francesco Procopio dei Coltelli, opened in Paris what many consider to be the first café, Il Procope. It quickly became the place where the literary and political glitterati of the day came to eat ices and other refreshments. Napoleon, Voltaire, Victor Hugo, Balzac and Benjamin Franklin were all patrons. Bedecked with mirrors, granite counter tops and chandeliers, Il Procope served as important community gathering place, a forerunner, of sorts, of the American ice cream parlour two centuries later.

Meanwhile, French confectioners were busy concocting frozen desserts – sometimes called *fromages*, not because they were made of cheese but because of the type of mould they were frozen in – from recipes they may have acquired during travels to Italy.

For example, Audiger in *La Maison reglée*, published the same year as Latini's *Lo scalco alla moderna*, describes making liquors and waters in the Italian style in flavours that included

'Les Glaces', engraving from an 18th-century series, *Le Bon genre* . . .

strawberry, raspberry and lemon. He also sketched out one brief recipe for ice cream, made with cream, sugar and orange flower water. (Sugar was an expensive rarity, first brought to Europe by the Italians from Arab areas in the Mediterranean and Middle East.)

Freezing techniques occupied another part of Audiger's book. To ensure that the flavours of his ices would stand up to the intense cold of the freezing process, Audiger instructed cooks to double the sugar and increase flavourings by half, Quinzio has explained.[7] And Audiger improved upon Latini's technique: he told cooks to stir the ices as they froze in order to create a fluffier texture.

The Early Ice Age

Creams, sorbets and flavourings were all critical to the development of modern ice creams. Yet another ingredient was crucial to ice cream's success – ice. Today, with modern refrigeration a given in most parts of the world, it's difficult for many to imagine ice as a luxury product. But for much of its history, ice was a costly, perishable extravagance, and remained so well into the nineteenth century.

The ancients – from Rome to China and Japan – had mastered the art of harvesting and storing ice. In Europe, Spanish and Italian nobility had ice brought down from mountains and stored it in pits to chill iced drinks and later for making sorbets. Early ice houses – pits covered in straw – also sprang up on the estates of the nobility in France and England in the sixteenth century. For example, the English King James 1 had two brick-lined snow pits dug in the ground at Greenwich between 1619 and 1622, according to Elizabeth David.[8]

Collecting and storing ice worked well enough for chilling drinks. But if the object was to use the ice to get food to freeze into a solid mass, that required additional ingenuity. The Chinese, the Arabs and the Indians all understood the principle of adding salt to ice to lower ice's temperature to below freezing. In this process, known as the endothermic effect, the cold in the ice and salt combination is transmitted to the ice cream mixture, freezing it solid.

Though the endothermic effect may seem like an obscure scientific concept more appropriate to the chemistry lab than to the kitchen, without it, ice cream would be little more than a melted puddle of flavoured cream. And without the discovery of the endothermic effect, there would be no ice cream as we know it today.

By the middle of the sixteenth century, Italian scientists had learned that submerging a container of water in a bucket of snow mixed together with potassium nitrate, or saltpeter, would freeze water solid. The saltpeter – later salt was used – lowered the freezing point of the ice, transferring heat from the ice cream mixture. Della Porta described this method of freezing wine in his 1559 text, *Natural Magick*, which was translated and which soon spread throughout Europe.

Meanwhile, ice cream travelled across the English Channel. In England, as in the rest of Europe, ice cream was a delicacy reserved for the high-born. King Charles II of England, for example, feasted on the frozen treat during a banquet that was staged for the Feast of St George at Windsor. The icy indulgence arrived at the King's table garnished with one gallon of red and two gallons of white strawberries.

By the eighteenth century, a prosperous middle class was beginning to emerge. To satisfy the demand for stylish desserts from English housewives, confectioners penned books filled with ice cream recipes. Across the Atlantic, ice cream was also making its debut. Still, when it came to ice cream innovation – from daring recipes to new freezing techniques – it was the Italians and French who continued to lead the way.

2

Confectioners and Colonists

I like the flavour very much
Of ice cream, but when it does touch
My tongue, quite paralysed I seem
At first, and afterwards ice cream!

from 'So Cold', anonymous, 1896

Italy and France, those bastions of pioneering iced desserts, continued well into the eighteenth century as centres of ice cream creativity. From an array of exotic new flavours, to advances in freezing methods, to the emergence of chic places to eat ice cream with groups of friends, to the addition of breadcrumbs and candies that foreshadowed today's 'mix-ins', early iced confections presaged future breakthroughs by Baskin-Robbins, Cold Stone Creamery and a host of other twenty-first-century brands. In 1775 a Neapolitan named Filippo Baldini produced *De'sorbetti*, the first book devoted entirely to the art of making frozen desserts, including sorbets flavoured with lemon and strawberry. Baldini also crafted confections enriched with pine nuts, pistachios, coffee, cinnamon and chocolate. And there was a recipe for 'milky sorbet', or ice cream, a creation that Baldini claimed possessed particularly impressive medical properties. A physician,

A French Sèvres porcelain 'refraichissoir' ice cream cooler from the 1760s.

Baldini ardently promoted iced desserts' multitude of health effects. For instance, he recommended cinnamon for relieving aches and pains, lemon ice cream for soothing ailing stomachs and chocolate to improve one's mood.

Around the same time that Baldini was unveiling his ice cream recipes, another Neapolitan, Vincenzo Corrado, an overseer of the kitchen, banquet and other household tasks of the city's wealthy, published recipes for more than thirty *sorbettos*. Flavours ranged from jasmine to pomegranate. There was also a recipe for an English custard, enriched with milk, cream, butter and cinnamon.[9]

The French Set the Style

Though the Italians continued to craft ice creams, the French also established themselves as trend-setters when it came to eighteenth-century frozen desserts. Whether called *fromages glacés*, *crème glace*, *neiges* or mousses, the aristocracy clamoured

An 18th-century ice cream vendor.

François Séraphin Delpech after Louis-Léopold Boilly, 'The Ice Cream Eaters', 1825, lithograph.

for ice cream. Ice cream was the exclusive preserve of the rich; one reason was that ingredients like sugar were very costly. Unlike today, when nearly every household cupboard stocks a bag of the sweetener, prudent eighteenth-century housewives kept their cache of sugar well secured under lock and key. Salt was pricey too, as were eggs and cream. Also driving up ice cream's cost were expensive spices and nuts, such as Middle Eastern rarities like pistachios, rosewater and almonds.

The lofty price of producing ice cream meant that only the affluent could purchase it. To satisfy the upper crust's craving, confectioners penned books brimming with recipes for ices and ice cream. For example, in 1768 a Frenchman

Frontispiece for M. Emy's *L'Art de bien faire les glaces d'office*, 1768. Emy concocted flavours ranging from avocado to foie gras.

named Monsieur Emy (we don't know his first name) published a compilation called *L'Art de bien faire les glaces d'office*. Emy offered up recipes for an array of ice cream flavours, including chocolate, artichoke, avocado, coffee, anise, violet, caramel, asparagus, foie gras and grated cheese. There was also vanilla, which today might seem a bit humdrum, but in Emy's day was considered quite exotic. Derived from the orchid plant, vanilla had arrived in Europe in the sixteenth century after being brought back from Mexico by Spanish explorers. (Perhaps this marrying of ingredients like vanilla from the Americas with European ice cream recipes was one of the earliest examples of ice cream's developing global profile.) Emy also strove to create texture in his ice cream.

Rye breadcrumbs were sprinkled atop his frozen creations, and cookies and candies were stirred into them as well.

In addition, Emy emphasized the importance of the mechanics of making ice cream. For example, he was very specific when it came to how to prepare a proper cream base. Making ice cream was not for the faint of heart. 'Stir the cream, as I've said, until it is thick, like a clear stew, even if it takes you an hour, because it's on this first step that the end result depends', he instructed. And Emy, like Baldini, lauded ice cream's health effects. To reap maximum benefit from the icy food, it should be served only in the summer, he suggested.

English Cookery Ladies

Across the channel in England, cookbook writers were aiming to teach the country's burgeoning middle class the fine points of ice cream making. One of ice cream's earliest English popularizers was Mrs Mary Eales, confectioner to Queen Anne. Her *Receipts*, first published in 1718, was the first cookbook in English to offer up a recipe. However, there wasn't much information for the aspiring ice cream maker, whether a servant or housewife, to go on. The only instruction she offered up to her readers was to fill tin pots 'with any sort of cream'. Pity the poor cook who required a refresher course on how to prepare a custard or cream.

Eales did describe in some detail the process of freezing ice cream. For example, she advised cooks to pack it in roughly twenty pounds of interwoven ice, straw and salt, making sure to 'cover the surface of the pot 'on every side. Set it in the Cellar where no Sun or Light comes; it will be froze in four hours', she assured her readers.

Soon, other English cookbook writers developed recipes for the new frozen cream. Among them was Hannah Glasse, who included a recipe for ice cream flavoured with raspberries – 'or whatever you like best' – in *The Art of Cookery Made Plain and Easy*, a popular book for home cooks first published in 1747. Glasse offered up brief instructions for making the dessert. One should take two pewter pots ('These things are made at the pewterers', she matter-of-factly told her readers) and put one inside the other. Her instructions for freezing a batch of ice cream were to the point:

> Fill [the bottom pot] with ice and a handful of salt. Let [the cream] stand in this ice three quarters of an hour, then uncover it and stir the cream well together. Cover it close again, and let it stand half an hour longer, after that, turn it onto your plate.

Almost as American as Apple Pie

As European settlers began to populate the New World, ice cream made its way onto the menus of upper-crust colonists. It's not certain when Americans first learned to make ice cream. Undoubtedly, the confectioners who set up shop in New York, Philadelphia and other colonial cities learned their craft from European counterparts. A number of English confectioners, for instance, had authored books that instructed housewives on the fine art of confectionery, including how to create biscuits, sweetmeats, ice creams and ices, which ranged in flavours from white coffee to pistachio and chocolate. One such instructor was Borella, who compiled *The Court and Country Confectioner; or, the House-Keeper's Guide* (1770). The former confectioner to the Spanish ambassador touted his

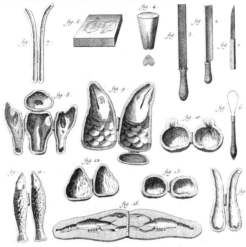

Tools and moulds for ice cream, from an edition of Diderot's *Encyclopaedia*.

impressive credentials, which included 'many years experience' abroad and in England serving as a confectioner 'in the homes of the most distinguished families'.

Frederick Nutt, another English confectioner, apparently borrowed liberally from Borella's recipes for his own work *The Complete Confectioner* (1789). Hostesses and their housekeepers could choose from nearly three dozen ice creams and two dozen water ice recipes. Extraordinarily rich by today's standards, one recipe called for ten egg yolks, two whole eggs and a pint of cream. To create a stylish display, Nutt, along with other confectioners of the time, recommended freezing ice

Thomas Jefferson's ice cream recipe, undated. The American president also constructed ice houses on his Virginia estate.

cream in moulds shaped like vegetables, animals and fruits. Pineapples, pears, apricots, asparagus, gherkins, truffles – even the head of a boar – were all popular presentations.

Meanwhile, in the American colonies, ice cream was gaining a foothold. One of the earliest Americans to consume ice cream was said to be William Black. Apparently, Black became an instant fan of the frozen treat. In 1700, while a guest of Maryland Governor Thomas Bladen, Black dined on 'some fine ice cream which, with the strawberries and milk, eat most deliciously'.

Founding Father Thomas Jefferson was another early American ice cream lover. He discovered the icy indulgence during his 1784 to 1789 tenure as US ambassador to France and brought a recipe back with him to Monticello. There, he made vanilla ice cream and served it to his guests. His recipe shows how time-consuming and arduous the task of making ice cream was. From gathering the ice to shaking the pails in which it was made, churning ice cream was no fun in the eighteenth century.

Like other well-to-do American and Europeans of the time, Jefferson erected ice houses – they held 62 wagonloads of ice – to store the ice that was harvested from a nearby river. Constructed to preserve meat and dairy, the ice houses also kept ice cream frozen and wine chilled.

The first president of the US, George Washington, was also an ice cream devotee. Inventory records for Mount Vernon, Washington's sprawling Virginia plantation, revealed that he owned two pewter ice cream pots, as well as several made of tin. In his diaries, Washington mentioned the backbreaking labour required to stock his ice house. 'Getting Ice as usual, which makes the 6th. day (except some interruption from the Weather on Tuesday) that as many people & Carts have been engaged in this work as could be advantageously employed', he wrote in February 1788 of the plantation's taxing ice-gathering activities.

When the new president was living in New York – the city served as the capital of the United States from 1785 until 1790 – he was apparently so fond of ice cream that during the sultry summer of 1790, Washington is said to have spent the princely sum of $200 to satisfy his yen. Around this time, the very first ice cream parlour was said to have opened in New York.

Ice cream quickly wrapped itself in a cloak of patriotism, as it became the treat of choice for Independence Day celebrations. In New York, on 4 July 1799, for example, citizens flocked to Vauxhall Gardens, a pleasure garden festooned with 'sixteen summer houses bearing the names of the 16 United States', a 20-foot (6 m) high grand temple of independence and coloured illuminations soaring eight feet high. Fireworks and rounds of cannon fire completed the festivities. Liquor, of course, flowed freely – along with peace officers to keep order among rowdy revellers. Another item that was served was ice cream. It was delicious. It was refreshing. It was the perfect food for cooling down overly exuberant celebrants on a hot July day. And ice cream signalled that an important celebration was taking place; it was a special food honouring the nation on its birthday.

At about the same time, cookbooks in America began to feature ice cream recipes. The first one said to have been published in the US was Richard Briggs's *The New Art of Cookery; According to the Present Practice Being a Complete Guide to All Housekeepers* (1792). Calling for a base of cream and sugar, Briggs' ice cream was flavoured with a dozen ripe apricots. (A nearly identical recipe had appeared in Mary Cole's *The Lady's Complete Guide*, or *Cookery in All its Branches*, published in London four years earlier.)

Other ice cream recipes followed. *Seventy-five Receipts for Pastry, Cakes, and Sweetmeats*, by 'A Lady of Philadelphia', first published in 1828, contained two ice cream recipes. One was a simple mixture of sugar and cream. Flavourings, advised the anonymous Lady, could range from lemon and almond to strawberry. The resulting conglomeration could be frozen in a mould, she suggested. The Lady's method for freezing the ice cream with salt and ice was strikingly similar to the one outlined by the English Mrs Eales. (Plagiarism was not unheard of among early cookbook writers and it's possible the Lady lifted her technique from Eales or from another English source.)

Yet another early ice cream tastemaker was African-American confectioner August Jackson. After working as a White House cook, Jackson moved to Philadelphia around 1832 and opened a catering business. There, he supplied the city's ice cream parlours with an assortment of ice cream flavours.

Enterprising Confectioners

Meanwhile, in New York, Boston, Philadelphia and other colonial towns, European confectioners were setting up shops to entice fashionable colonials to purchase ice cream. Cities like late eighteenth-century New York were veritable beehives of ice cream making and retailing activity. In the years before the Revolutionary War, New York confectioners competed aggressively to promote their wares and undersell competitors with that same money-hungry zeal that characterizes business activity in the city today. For instance, Londoner Philip Lenzi, who had emigrated to New York, placed an advertisement in the November 1773 *Rivington's New York Gazetteer* designed to generate buzz for the opening of his new shop at No. 517 Hanover. There, he said, customers could purchase a full range of sweets: jams, jellies, 'all sorts of sugar plums', white and brown sugar candy, fruits and ice cream. Lenzi promoted the quality and especially the price of his goods. Declared the confectioner: their quality displayed 'the greatest perfection'. And, he reassured his customers, all 'would be sold at the most reasonable rates'.

Other confectioners soon flocked to the area, which we know today as the bustling financial centre of Wall Street. There was Peter Laune at 54 Wall Street, who proclaimed the superior quality of his ice cream. Then there was A. Pryor, just up the street at 59 Wall, and Frenchman Joseph Corre, who bounced around a bit before settling at 55 Wall. Vallette and Company, confectioners and distillers from Rouen, France, announced the availability of bonbons and sugar almonds, sugar in sticks and tablets, apple, currant and quince jellies and fruit preserved in brandy. Ice cream was on the menu as well. 'They likewise inform the public that they will make every day, ice cream of all tastes', an ad for his establishment declared.

Confectioneries were springing up from Boston to Philadelphia. The enterprising New York confectioner Corre set up a shop in Philadelphia in 1795, where, he advised prospective customers, they could purchase his ice cream for 'the moderate price of 11 pence per glass'. Thanks to a high concentration of dairy farms that ringed the city, Philadelphia became a centre of ice cream making, producing a distinctive variety consisting of cream, sugar and flavourings, but no eggs.

Early American rural ice cream stand, *Lippincott's Magazine*, 1877. The print emphasizes the ice cream class divide – cheap hokey pokey ices for the poor, while the upper-crust crowd stands off in the distance.

Ice Cream Travels to the Hinterlands

Ice cream was still a fairly uncommon treat, but around the turn of the century it started to show up in everyday American dining establishments. American coffee houses, taverns and saloons lured customers with the promise of ice cream on the menu. A Philadelphia tavern called The City of Hamburg announced that its cooks prepared ice cream fresh every single day. Innkeepers began to stock ice cream, promoting the icy confection as the perfect balm to soothe weary travellers. Candy and other treats were sold alongside it. An 1840s Cincinnati confectioner's menu of soda water, mead (a honey wine), lemonade, candies and nuts and ice cream was typical. Women as well as men operated saloons and catering establishments and many got into the ice cream business. One who advertised her frozen treats was L.A.W. Pyle of West Chester, Pennsylvania, who offered to deliver her exceptional and well-priced ice cream – it 'far surpasses anything of the kind we have ever tasted', she declared – to local households 'at a very trifling cost'.

In nearby Wilmington, Delaware, a freed black slave known as Aunt Sallie Shadd was acclaimed for the excellent quality of her ice cream. The story goes that Dolly Madison, wife of US President James Madison, travelled to Wilmington to sample the treat, which the First Lady then famously served at the White House.

It wasn't long before ice cream travelled to remote frontier areas. Some country folks reacted with alarm at the startling and entirely new sensation of ingesting ice-cold food, newspapers of the day reported. But the era of mass-produced ice cream was dawning. Soon, the frozen confection would become the dessert choice of rich and poor alike.

3
Ice Cream for the Masses

In summer ice-cream and soda-water
Do please the maidens all;
But then in the winter they think a man
Oughter escort them to the ball.

Anonymous, 1833

When in 1862 Mrs Henrietta Hall opened a saloon just west of the courthouse square in Media, Pennsylvania, her ice cream drew raves from the local newspaper, the *Delaware County Republican*. 'We willingly commend the excellent quality of her cream to the attention of the lovers of this special summer luxury', gushed the anonymous reviewer.

At the time that Mrs Hall was being acclaimed for the quality of her ice cream, the food barely existed as a commercial product in US, or anywhere else in the world for that matter. In 1859, a total of 4,000 gallons (15,000 litres) were produced in the entire US, according to an International Association of Ice Cream Vendors history of the ice cream industry.

But all that was about to change, ushering in a period when ice cream would evolve from an expensive luxury into an affordable mass-market product. Just ten years before Mrs Hall was complimented for her ice cream, Philadelphian

Nancy Johnson had received a patent for her revolutionary mechanical ice cream-making machine, a device that would vastly speed up the process of churning the frozen confection and usher in the era of mass manufacturing of the product. A decade later, Jacob Fussell, a Baltimore dairy man, would become the first to produce ice cream on a commercial scale, opening factories up and down the eastern seaboard of the US.

What about the Italians and French, who had done so much to advance the culinary art and science of ice cream making? In those countries, as in much of the rest of Europe, ice cream artisans operated on a small scale. Parents handed down their ice cream-making recipes to sons and daughters. English inventors did roll out their own mechanized ice cream-making machines at about the same time as Johnson, but it wasn't until the end of the early years of the twentieth century, with the expansion of English food company Wall's into the ice cream business, that full-scale commercialization of the product took hold in the British Isles.

What explains the Americans' competitive edge when it came to commercial ice cream production? Americans certainly lacked Europeans' culinary polish. Yet New World entrepreneurial spirit led to technological, product development and marketing breakthroughs that transformed ice cream into a worldwide consumer dessert staple. Simply put, for American ice cream makers, the dessert offered a business opportunity – even more than a culinary challenge.

Cranking and Churning

Johnson's mechanical ice cream machine, which received a patent in 1843, paved the way for the growth of the commercial ice cream industry, not just in the US, but eventually worldwide. Before Johnson, preparing ice cream was a gruelling task that extracted hours from a cook's day. Using the pot freezer method, cooks would place the sugar, cream and flavourings into a container, which in turn was fitted into a pail filled with an ice and salt mixture. Shaking the cream and flavourings up and down while beating the cream and scraping it from the sides of the container, cooks would spend long hours whipping and beating it into a frozen state.

Clearly, if ice cream were ever to be produced in bulk, the process would need to be streamlined. That's where the American Johnson entered the picture. By mechanizing the process with a crank that turned a dasher that scraped and churned the cream, she transformed ice cream production from a backbreaking chore into an efficient process. Now, it was possible to move ice cream making from the confectionary shop into the factory.

Little is known about Johnson other than the fact that she won a US patent (3254) on 9 September 1843 for her hand-cranked ice cream maker. Accompanying the application for her new 'artificial freezer' is a simple line drawing of the device and a careful explanation of how it would work. In the written part of her application, Johnson pitched her new device as a significant labour-saving advance. No longer would 'the hands of the operator' be forced to spend hours manually stirring and scraping ice cream. From now on, all that was required of a cook was to give the crank several good turns. That action would turn the dasher, ferrying the ingredients from the edge of the freezer to the centre and back again, 'thus constantly allowing fresh portions of the cream or other substances to be frozen to come in contact with the refrigerating surface'.

In England, inventor Thomas Masters unveiled his own labour-saving ice cream-making device. In his 1840

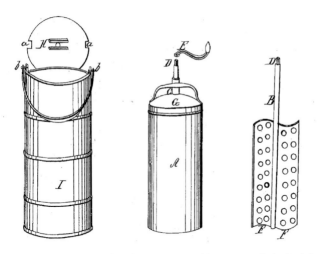

Nancy M. Johnson's 'artificial freezer', patented in 1843, revolutionized the ice cream industry, paving the way for its eventual mass production.

compendium, *The Ice Book*, Masters, a born salesman, argued that the pot freezer method was seriously out of date, unnecessarily time-consuming and difficult to execute. Moreover, the ice cream that resulted from the pot freezer process produced an inferior product, claimed Masters, because the 'delicate' ice cream would be 'spoiled' for 'want of proper beating up'. Instead, Masters recommended his new artificial ice-producing invention – composed of two wooden pails, a metal freezer and a crank, which cooks could easily turn to produce a nicely churned frozen dessert.

To promote his new machine – Masters received a patent for his device the same year as Johnson – the English inventor enlisted a marketing ploy, one that today's kitchen equipment manufacturers would surely appreciate. He embellished his book with scores of ice cream recipes that were designed to be prepared specifically using his newfangled mechanical ice cream maker. There were recipes for vanilla, ginger, apricot, pineapple and brown bread ice cream. But what should the thrifty housewife do with all that leftover ice? Masters proposed a solution for that, too. Turn it into ice sculptures, 'like a castle turret' for glittering adornments suitable for sideboards and dining-room tables, he suggested.

In the second half of the nineteenth century, manufacturers came up with increasingly sophisticated ice cream makers that were capable of churning out thousands of gallons of the frozen treat. Some were electrically driven while others were powered by steam. But without the inventions of Johnson and Masters, ice cream would have remained a craft product. Meanwhile, a man emerged who would harness the power of new technology to manufacture ice cream and sell it to the masses.

A Manufactured Dessert

It was one thing to ease the arduous task of churning ice cream by hand and to make it more efficient. But it took the business acumen of a dairy wholesaler, Jacob Fussell of Baltimore, to envision the way in which ice cream could be manufactured on a large scale. He was able to increase output and cut the price, this making the delicacy more widely available to the masses.

Faced with a surplus of cream during the summer months, Fussell decided to take the excess and turn it into ice cream. His first factory opened in Pennsylvania around 1851, where, according to an account in the *Washington InSider*, he made his ice cream with manually operated churns. He then moved his operations to Baltimore. It wasn't long before the ice cream entrepreneur – who consistently undersold his competitors – was operating plants all along the Eastern seaboard, with operations in Washington, DC, Boston and New York. Fussell was apparently able to amass some wealth from his ice cream manufacturing enterprise. In 1914, two years after his death at age 93, the *New York Times* reported that the magnate had 'made a fortune in ice cream', and that among his assets were $1,993 in cash, shares of stock in coal and steel companies, and $10,000 in life insurance.

Others, sniffing out money-making opportunities, also invested in the ice cream business in the years following the American Civil War. (In England, meanwhile, some small-scale manufacturing took place. By 1858, a Swiss-Italian café owner and ice merchant named Carlo Gatti was turning out thousands of penny ices.) One of Fussell's partners, James Madison Horton, bought him out and established the J. M. Horton Ice Cream Company in 1874. William Breyer, who opened his first ice cream shop in Philadelphia in 1882, had set up a wholesale manufacturing plant by the turn of the century. By 1918, according to the Breyers company website, Breyers was churning out more than a million gallons (3.8 million litres) of ice cream a year and shipping its product to customers in cities like New York and Washington, DC.

Do the Hokey Pokey

Other changes were occurring, starting around the middle of the nineteenth century, that would also help transform the making and selling of ice cream. In Italy, political turmoil rocked the country, sparking the migration of large numbers of Italians to other parts of Europe, such as Germany and Holland, and to the US. Plagued by extreme poverty, these immigrants were also seeking better economic opportunities. But many wound up in subsistence street jobs in their new homes. Some became organ grinders. Others, however, took up the occupation of ice cream making and vending. Known as hokey pokey vendors, these immigrant hawkers pushed carts through the streets of cities like London, Glasgow and New York, selling cheap glasses full of 'hokey pokey' to children and adults. Thus was the ice cream treat as cheap street food born. Almost anyone could afford the inexpensive frozen street snack. Children and adults clamoured for it.

By the latter half of the nineteenth century, cities throughout Europe and in the US were flooded with these itinerant ice cream vendors. About 4,000 Italians migrated to Scotland from Italy between 1890 and the Second World War, according to Alastair Gray's *A History of Scotland*, and many of them sold ice cream. And by the late nineteenth century, there were about 20,000 Italian ice cream sellers and organ grinders working in London. In Germany, Italians also sold ice cream from carts. Today, gelato stands dot street corners in Berlin and in other German cities, a legacy from that earlier time when Italian immigrants sold cheap ice cream throughout the country.

In New York, hokey pokey men were observed selling ice cream as early as 1828; by 1901, there were 4,000 hokey pokey hawkers 'turned loose on the streets' of the city, as one contemporary press report put it.

Whether in Glasgow, Berlin or New York, the proprietors of these forerunners of today's ice cream vans and trucks would call out, '*Gelati, ecco un poco*' or 'ice creams, here a little'. The origins of the term 'hokey pokey' are obscure. Some say it's a corruption of 'hocus pocus'. Others maintain that 'hokey pokey' is an English interpretation of an Italian phrase, '*o che pocco*' for 'oh so little', which could have referred to the inexpensive price of the watery ice cream they sold.

Children loved the cheap 'half-penny ices' the Italian immigrant hokey pokey vendors sold across the British isles, 1876–7.

Loaded up with their frosty wares – it was more like ice milk than ice cream – vendors shouted out their cry:

Hokey-pokey, pokey ho. Hokey-pokey, a penny a lump.
Hokey-pokey, find a cake; hokey-pokey on the lake.
Here's the stuff to make you jump;
Hokey-pokey, penny a lump.
Hokey-pokey, sweet and cold;
For a penny, new or old.

Wrapping a block of ice cream in paper or filling a small glass with it, hokey pokey vendors would sell a 'lick' for about a penny, then wipe the glass out for the next paying client. '[T]he street *gamins* and errand boys buzz around their barrows like flies about a sugar barrel', wrote London chronicler Andrew W. Tuer in his 1897 publication *Cries*. 'For obvious reasons, spoons are not lent', he added. 'The soft and half-frozen delicacy is consumed by the combined aid of tongue and fingers.'

Living and working conditions for the ice cream sellers were described by contemporary observers as appalling. Many vendors were forced to inhabit squalid neighbourhoods 'in no way dissimilar from a London slum', as one writer put it. Not surprisingly, concerns about sanitation dogged hokey pokey men on both sides of the Atlantic. In 1901 the New York publication *Medical News* reported that the city of Brighton, England had imposed fines on street vendors who were accused of selling contaminated ice cream that regularly made customers ill. Five years later, the Pennsylvania Department of Agriculture was sounding the alarm about unsanitary ice cream vending in Philadelphia.

But despite occasional health scares, many hokey pokey sellers managed to prosper. In fact, some vendors went on to establish thriving ice cream concerns. Exeter, England native Anthony Edmund Forte told of the 'ice cream wars' that broke out among the town's hokey pokey vendors – several of whom were Forte's ancestors – in the early years of the twentieth century. Eventually, the family prospered, moving from street vending to operating an ice cream factory called D. Forte & Sons.

Not every Italian immigrant with a penchant for ice cream making became a street vendor. Some time around 1890, confectioner Angelo Brocato immigrated to New Orleans from Sicily, where he had worked as a confectioner in three well-known Palermo gelaterias. In Sicily, Anthony had learned how to 'pick nuts for the gelato and shovel ice and salt', recalled his grandson, Arthur Brocato, who today still turns out gelato and classic Italian cookies and candies at the family's bustling ice cream parlour in New Orleans' Midtown section. Working initially in the sugar cane fields of southern Louisiana, patriarch Angelo accumulated enough money to open his first New Orleans shop in 1905. Churning ice cream by hand, the Sicilian gelato maker produced treats like Torroncino, a vanilla-based gelato with cinnamon and ground almonds; lemon ice; and spumoni, the multi-flavoured moulded confection made of layers of ice cream, fruits, nuts and whipped cream.

Nor was every ice cream merchant Italian. Mary Antin, in *The Promised Land* (1912), her account of her Jewish immigrant family's life in Boston at the turn of the twentieth century, wrote about how her father sold ice cream when she was a child at a nearby seaside resort. 'He dished out ice cream with enthusiasm, so I supposed he was getting rich', recalled Anton of her father's operation, which never generated the hoped-for wealth.

Keep it Cool

It was becoming easier and quicker to make ice cream. There were wholesalers now in a position to distribute it in large quantities. And there were street peddlers eager to sell ice cream cheaply to all comers – from street urchins to families enjoying a day of relaxation at a city park or a beach-side resort. But another challenge remained – cutting and shipping enough ice from frozen lakes and ponds to satisfy the mounting demand for ice cream.

Entrepreneurs sensed a business opportunity, and soon the ice trade was experiencing explosive growth. In the first half of the nineteenth century, New England ice barons such as Frederick Tudor, known as the 'Ice King', Charles Wyman Morse and Nathaniel Wyeth harvested and shipped millions of tons of ice from the world's cold regions. Norway in Europe and New England in the US were two fertile ice-producing regions that shipped the refrigerant to ice-hungry citizens from London to Calcutta. And trading in ice was highly profitable. In 1886, at the peak of the natural ice boom,

These ice houses near Lexington, Kentucky, built *c.* 1830, were typical of the structures erected to store ice harvested from nearby rivers and lakes.

Men harvesting ice with saws, between 1900 and 1910.

over 25 million tons of ice were harvested in the United States alone. One Ohio company announced that during the winter of 1899 it would be shipping 2,000 rail cars of ice – about 50,000 tons – to its customers. In England, the ice business flourished as well. A Liverpool facility announced that it was expanding to one million cubic feet of cold storage in order to hold an expected inventory of 50 tons of ice a day.

By the end of the nineteenth century, Morse was raking in an astonishing $60 million from his ice enterprise. Clearly, ice – and ice cream – were emerging as big money-makers for some enterprising businessmen. And ice cream was being eaten by growing numbers of ordinary citizens. But it would take the ice cream soda fountain – and the treats that it spawned – to broaden ice cream's appeal even further. Now, special dining establishments – parlours and soda fountains – would spring up in nearly every community in the us, solely for the purpose of serving the luscious treat. Ice cream was becoming a middle-class staple, eaten and enjoyed by all segments of society.

4
Ice Cream's Golden Age

Something New!

Green's Ice Cream Soda

The Most Delicious Drink

Drawn from R. M. Green's Block Tin-Lined

Steel Fountain . . .

Lemon, Vanilla, Pineapple, Strawberry, Raspberry,

Ginger, Sarsaparilla, Nectar, Orange . . .

Ten Cents a Glass

Try it and Tell all Your Friends

Robert Green's 1874 flyer announcing his new ice cream soda creation

Dating back to the courts of the ancient Chinese emperors and to the banquet halls of European aristocracy, ice cream remained for centuries a luxury beyond the reach of ordinary citizens. But with technological advances beginning in the mid-nineteenth century, and with the widespread emergence of street vendors, regular folks could now, finally, scrounge up a few pennies to buy an ice cream.

Scholars agree that starting in the years after the Civil War and stretching well into the early decades of the twentieth century, American ice cream entrepreneurs ushered in a veritable golden age of ice cream innovation. It was the age of the soda fountain – that uniquely American community gathering spot where ice cream was gobbled up and gossip was exchanged in nearly equal measure. It was the age of the ice cream cone, of the ice cream sundae, of the ice cream soda and of the ice cream bar on a stick. These items were delicious. They were inexpensive. Many were portable, made to be consumed while walking down the street, or on a beach or at an amusement park outing. Most importantly, these new frozen creations spelled fun. On a hot summer's day, a cone or a soda was irresistible.

And when it came to manufacturing and retailing ice cream, America's primacy was widely acknowledged – not just in the US, but in Europe as well. By the mid-nineteenth century, Europeans were conceding that America was the 'land of ice cream', as ice cream historian Jeri Quinzio has

An engraving of a mid-nineteenth-century Italian sorbet seller, *c.* 1850s. Italian gelato makers handed down the craft of gelato-making to their children, producing the delicacy in small quantities for local consumption.

An Italian gelato-seller, *c.* 1934.

put it.[10] 'European confectioners began to look across the Atlantic for ideas', she has written. 'America now set the standard.' Meanwhile, the Italians, the originators of modern ice cream, were ill equipped to spearhead the drive to commercialize ice cream. Their refrigeration techniques lagged, and Italian gelato – which means 'frozen' in Italian – was hand-made, batch by batch. Though lower in butterfat than large-batch commercial ice cream, gelato was a dense, rich confection. Gelato also contained less air than conventional ice cream. But the fact that individual families of artisans continued to produce gelato and *sorbetto* – rather than large-scale factories – meant that these confections remained a regional speciality until very recently. In fact, most Italian ice cream makers, even if they had wanted to engage in mass market production, lacked the funds to invest in new refrigeration and other advances until well into the twentieth century.[11] (For modern gelato production, see pp. 121–3.)

To be sure, the quality of even the best American ice cream – its taste, texture and richness – couldn't begin to match that of gelato. But while Americans may have fallen down on the culinary side, they excelled when it came to producing and merchandizing ice cream for the masses. And American consumers' seemingly insatiable appetite for ice cream helped fuel the business's success. '[N]owadays, no American expects or receives less than a heaping saucer of ice cream at a time,' wrote Englishman Fullarton Muirhead during his 1890s travels through America.

Soda Fountains Everywhere

By the end of the nineteenth century, fountains and parlours by the thousands honeycombed the US, popping up in drugstores, department stores, railroad cars – even in bowling alleys. Though Americans continued to make ice cream at home or to purchase it from confectioners, soda fountains soon dominated the ice cream landscape; they were *the* preferred venue for consuming ice cream outside the home. 'The United States is the greatest soda fountain country in the world', the *New York Times* proclaimed in a 1916 story, which pegged the combined retail value of fountain treats at a staggering $500 million.

How did these establishments – enshrined in countless Hollywood films as the embodiment of small town American values – get their start? And what explains their potent allure?

Like so many other 'American' ice cream institutions, soda fountains trace their roots to distant locales. Drinking bubbly water was fashionable in both Europe and the Far East. There, mineral waters – sought after for their supposed curative powers – bubbled up from natural springs. Soon, scientists

Soda fountain at Zaharakos Ice Cream Parlor, 329 Washington Street, Columbus, Indiana, *c.* 1910. Still operated by the Zaharakos family, this 110-year-old ice-cream parlour served for years as the town's social centre and boasted oak wall panels with ornate wood carvings, two Mexican onyx soda fountains, a Tiffany lamp and a pipe organ.

across Europe were embarking on a quest to imbue water artificially by means of carbonation. By the early 1770s, both Swedish chemist Torbern Bergman and English scientist Joseph Priestley had discovered how to infuse water with carbon dioxide. In 1807 Englishman Henry Thompson received a patent for infusing water with carbon dioxide. The newfangled beverage was dubbed 'soda water' and was pumped out of an apparatus.

It wasn't long before carbonated water made its way across the Atlantic. By the first decade of the nineteenth century, pharmacists in Philadelphia, New York and elsewhere were dispensing the effervescent liquid to eager customers. Since soda water was believed to possess therapeutic properties, druggists, as dispensers of medical remedies, were the logical purveyors of the fizzy drink. Adding flavours like lemon and vanilla to the water boosted the already sought-after refreshment's popularity to even greater heights.

The invention of machines specially designed to pump out soda water under pressure also propelled the growth of soda fountains. At first, soda water was forced through goose-neck-shaped spigots. In 1832 Englishman John Matthews immigrated to New York, where he established a business manufacturing machines designed especially to push out the water. (At around that time, 'Old Ben', a freed slave who worked for Matthews, opened perhaps the earliest New York establishment for dispensing soda water at 55 Gold Street.) Other soda fountain machine pioneers – A. D. Puffer of Boston, John Lippincott of Philadelphia and Boston drug-gist James W. Tufts, among them – crafted box-shaped contrivances from marble, iron or copper; they were designed to sit on a drugstore counter. Soon, the contraptions evolved into masterpieces of extravagant design. Turned out in an array of forms that mimicked modish Romantic and neoclas-sical architectural styles of the days – swans, cottages, tombs, temples, lions, sphinxes and urns were all popular – soda fountains were crafted to wow pharmacy customers.

To market their flashy new contrivances, soda fountain manufacturers sought ways to showcase them. At the 1876 Centennial Exhibition in Philadelphia, Lippincott and Tufts paid the extravagant sum of $50,000 to furnish the fair with fourteen fountains, all of which were festooned with angels, gilding, silver pillars and urns. Tufts also erected a marble and silver soda water machine that soared more than 30 feet (9 m) over the fairgrounds. It turned out that this deft marketing manoeuvre paid handsome dividends. The public was awe-struck, and soon druggists were clamouring for them. Tufts's and Lippincott's showmanship helped propel the industry forward and it wasn't long before elaborate soda fountains became fixtures in pharmacies across America.

By the last quarter of the nineteenth century, druggists had figured out that adding ice cream to soda was a winning combination. And before long, druggists started to designate separate areas in their pharmacies as 'soda fountains'. These were places specifically set aside for patrons to feast on ice cream treats, either while sitting at a table or perched on a stool at a long marble counter. Behind the counter, the druggist and his ice cream-treat-making employee, the white-uniformed soda jerk, would create fountain favourites for a steady stream of ice cream-crazy patrons. 'Elegant fixtures, a grand soda fountain, chairs and handsome tables filling up the center of the store' adorned one such fountain, wrote an observer in the 1901 edition of the trade journal, *Meyer Brothers Druggist*. From christenings to graduations, from ladies' gatherings to teen get-togethers – the soda fountain had arrived and was fully embraced by kids and adults alike.

Theodore Stanley Krzywinski, who operated a Chicago sweet shop with a soda fountain from 1948 to 1967, recently recalled:

> The soda fountain was the heart of the business. There was a marble counter with six stools and a round mirror and shelves behind the bar. There were five booths in the back of the store and a jukebox so teens would come in to eat ice cream creations and dance the jitterbug.

By 1900, drugstore soda fountains were said to outnumber saloons. The *New York Times* estimated in 1916 that 100,000 fountains dotted the US, with half residing in drugstores and another quarter in confectionary shops. And the importance of soda fountains exceeded the delicious treats

A postcard of Becker's Ice Cream Parlor and its white-uniformed staff, New York, 1900.

served there. A quintessential 'third place' – a neighbourhood establishment that local citizens gravitate to for fellowship and community – the drugstore soda fountain 'was unoccupied only rarely and never when school let out', reported Ray Oldenburg in his study of American small towns, *The Great Good Place*.[12] 'Without question, the drugstore was the most preferred third place or hangout.'

Soda fountains doubled as small town economic engines, creating expanded business opportunities for druggists and confectioners. With the installation of a fountain, a druggist could instantly broaden his product line beyond pills and potions to sodas and sundaes. Drugstore trade publications fuelled the trend, declaring that a diligent soda fountain operator, if he played his cards right, could easily count on a

US pharmacists expanded their businesses by installing soda fountains in their shops. Soon, they became all the rage. Anna Louise James (1886–1977), shown here behind the soda fountain of her drugstore, was the first woman pharmacist in Connecticut.

steady stream of profits. A merchant with just a couple of thousand customers could bring in 'fifteen hundred to two thousand dollars a year with a net profit of thirty-three and one-third per cent,' wrote druggist Jesse L. Nelson in a 1909 article. Other soda fountain proselytizers also laid out a road-map to profitability. Take care of your equipment, keep tabs on the competition, train the help well and position the soda fountain machine in a highly visible spot, advised Brooklyn pharmacist Milo E. Mendenhall in the 1920 edition of the trade journal *Bulletin of Pharmacy*. Mendenhall insisted that the enterprising druggist was practically guaranteed a steady flow of revenues. 'The public has the money and is ready to spend it', he declared.

And spend it they did. One turn-of-the-century New York establishment reported selling out of 100 gallons (380 litres) of ice cream and 9,000 lb (4,080 kg) of ice in a single day. And

An aerial view of the interior of Peoples Drug Store soda fountain taken some time between 1909 and 1932. This shop was located in Washington, DC's central business district. A local institution, Peoples was bought out by another concern in 1994.

when the Volstead Act ushered in Prohibition in 1920, soda fountains' popularity vaulted to new heights. Saloons were shuttered and reconfigured into fountains and parlours. St Louis brewer Anheuser-Busch was among the many beer makers that switched to making ice cream. Hotels and cafés converted bars to soda fountains and ice cream parlours. Socializing can occur 'as well over temperance drinks and soda fountain products as over the real thing', wrote Albert Pick and Company, a firm of Chicago hotel outfitters, in one of its marketing brochures. Since saloons were shuttered, men drifted into soda fountains in growing numbers. Still, for many beer-drinking men who had inhabited saloons and bars, adapting to the new order wasn't always easy. Only 'little girls and dudes drink ice cream and soda', sniffed one chagrined fellow to a *Chicago Tribune* reporter.

By the time Prohibition came to an end in 1933, soda fountains had sprouted in nearly every American city and town. And entire industries blossomed because of the soda fountain trade. Wood carving and leaded glass work, not to mention fruit preserving and syrup-making, all benefited from the fountains' spread across the US.

In Europe and the Far East, the fountain fad was slower to take hold. A drugstore soda fountain opened in the Ginza district of Tokyo in 1900, 'imitating the American drugstore', according to a Japanese Ice Cream Association history of ice cream in Japan. In England, American soldiers passing through on their way to First World War battlefields across the channel crowded English soda fountains. The country's cool, wet weather had hobbled fountains' growth; many English ice cream lovers considered ice cream strictly a warm-weather snack. Soon, however, fountains, and along with them, treats

Though ice cream parlours and soda fountains were primarily an American institution, they caught on around the world. This Tokyo department store featured an elaborate one in the 1920s.

like sodas and sundaes, began to catch on. 'The circumstance is all the more remarkable when it is considered that the fountain apparatus, the syrups, sodas, and sundaes as well as the basic habit of drinking fountain products are all of American origin', proclaimed the trade magazine *Soda Fountain*, which reported in 1921 that a London opera house had erected an opulent version of the American import. Villages and towns across England installed fountains, too. Though the number of English fountains never approached those gracing US cities and towns, the English eventually embraced the new dining establishments. At Selfridges department store in London, which installed an elaborate fountain, 'the crowd at the fountain started at the opening time and the doors had to be locked when the time came to close the store', wrote one observer. Other department stores – Levin's in Liverpool and Harrods in London were just two examples – also jumped on the soda fountain bandwagon. Tea shops and restaurants also rolled out fountain treats.

The Ice Cream Soda

At the heart of the soda fountain's appeal, of course, were the delicious – and eye-catching – ice cream treats served there. Though sundaes, milk shakes and other fountain concoctions had their fans, for many customers, a trip to the soda fountain wasn't complete unless it included the chance to slurp down a frothy ice cream soda.

It wasn't until the late nineteenth century that two men – no one knows who came up with the idea first – conjured up the idea of mixing soda water with ice cream. One possible inventor was Robert Green. Green sold flavoured soda water at the 1874 semi-centennial celebration in Philadelphia. He

A dextrous soda jerk flipping ice cream into malted milk shakes, 1939.

A Wisconsin soda jerk stands behinds a typical mid-century serpentine counter in the Bancroft Dairy fountain room while his customers tuck into ice cream treats, 1937.

ran out of the cream he typically used to flavour the drinks. As the story goes, he infused the soda with ice cream instead. Soon, the new treat became a runaway sensation. In another version of the soda creation tale, at around the same time that Green was launching his new drinkable ice cream treat, Detroit drugstore owner Fred Sanders found that his stock of cream had turned sour. He, too, flavoured his bubbly water with ice cream.

Regardless of who actually invented the ice cream soda, the liquid fountain treats soon exploded into a *bona fide* national craze. In the US, ice cream sodas were the centrepiece of soda fountain and ice cream parlour menus. Composed of soda water, a scoop or two of ice cream and chocolate, strawberry or other flavourings, ice cream sodas were both eaten with a spoon and sipped through a straw. Teenage soda jerks assembled the fountain treats, displaying their dexterity by flamboyantly squirting arcs of soda water into a glass into which a scoop or two of ice cream had been artfully placed.

Constructing an ice cream soda was a feat of culinary derring-do. So elaborate and intricate was the routine that druggists' manuals devoted huge amounts of space to the proper execution of an ice cream soda. The 1897 *Standard Manual of Soda and Other Beverages* was typical: '[P]ut about 1 to 2 fluid ounces of syrup into the glass,' the instructions stated, then 'turn in the fine stream of carbonated water, moving the glass about quickly so that the stream may play upon every portion of the syrup in the glass.' The manual then detailed at great length the intricate choreography required for assembling the perfect ice cream soda.

Soda jerks flung around their own special lingo to describe their fountain theatrics. For instance, a 'bucket of hail' was ice, a 'house boat' was a banana split, and 'suds' was root beer. The teenage ice cream jockeys were hometown celebrities. Even mobsters paid homage to them. One, notorious gangster Meyer Lansky, staged an annual face-off in which soda jerks from all five New York boroughs created black and tan ice cream sodas (made with coffee ice cream and chocolate syrup) at a Bronx soda fountain. Not surprisingly, the soda-making bout was rigged, with the winner predictably a Lansky protégé.[13]

Throughout the late nineteenth century and well into the middle of the twentieth, recipes for ice cream sodas proliferated. There were banana, cherry, chocolate, cantaloupe and maple ones. There was the 'black cow', a confection made with vanilla ice cream, root beer and chocolate syrup; the 'purple cow', composed of ginger ale, vanilla ice cream and grape juice; and the Boston Cooler, a mixture of vanilla ice cream and ginger ale. Soda fountains also turned out milk shakes and malteds – thick drinks made with ice cream and milk, then whirred in a blender. (Today, bourbon, vodka

The Cream of Love, c. 1879. This Currier and Ives print, depicting two winged cherubs eating a very large dish of ice cream, lavishly illustrates late 19th-century Americans' passion for eating the frozen dessert.

and even beer are the cutting-edge syrups used for making sodas that while intended for grown-ups also evoke sweet childhood memories.)

Sodas were capable of inspiring near rhapsodic reactions. One 1880s Omaha newspaper writer enthused that the ice cream soda was nothing less than 'a drink that combines one ice cream and one soda in a moonlight sonata of perfect harmony'. And Americans appeared to agree. By 1913, over 475 million gallons (1.8 billion litres) of soda water were consumed annually in the US alone.

The Sundae

One of the great dessert innovations of all time, the sundae – a near-perfect rhapsody of sauce, ice cream and whipped cream – came into being in the early 1890s. The French had the coupé – ice cream sauced with fruit and other toppings – and even Americans ate ice cream with toppings before the sundae was officially born. But the modern sundae came about, as one story goes, because blue laws in some American towns banned the sale of ice cream sodas on Sundays, considered too frivolous to be consumed on the Sabbath. What to do? Dish up ice cream and sauce – minus the soda water. Thus was the sundae created, or at least that's one version of the tale.

Even today, more than a hundred years later, the question of who invented the ice cream sundae continues to inspire fierce civic rivalries. Some give the nod to a druggist in Ithaca, New York; others to a proprietor in Two Rivers, Wisconsin. Buffalo, New York and Evanston, Illinois also have staked claims to the delicious dessert. For years, Two Rivers and Ithaca have engaged in a spirited (but friendly) debate over which town should be crowned the official sundae birthplace. Ithaca, in fact, maintains that it can produce an advertisement featured in an April 1892 edition of the *Ithaca Daily Journal* describing a cherry ice cream sundae.

In Ithaca's account, local pastor Reverend John M. Scott stopped by the Platt & Colt Pharmacy after Sunday services for his usual dish of vanilla ice cream. That day, instead of plain vanilla, Platt dressed up a scoop of ice cream with cherry sauce and a candied cherry. The two discussed what to name the dish and decided to call it the 'sundae' after the day of the week on which it had been first concocted.

Regardless of who actually originated the dish, the decadent snack took the us by storm. Women, in particular, craved the dish. Schrafft's, an American restaurant chain that catered to a female clientele, paired ladylike dishes like lobster Newburg with hot fudge sundaes for dessert.

By the beginning of the twentieth century, confectioners, soda fountain operators and drugstore soda fountain manuals had spawned countless variations of the popular sundae. Toppings included hot fudge, marshmallow, strawberry and caramel sauces, not to mention even more fanciful confections incorporating nuts, candy, and fruits. Among them were the George Washington (a scoop of vanilla ice cream, garnished with six maraschino cherries, whipped cream and a sprinkle of crushed roasted almonds); the Over the Top (two scoops of vanilla ice cream, a piece of nougat candy, maple syrup and whipped cream); and the County Cork (orange-flower water syrup coloured a light green, pistachio ice cream, crystallized ginger, roasted filberts, whipped cream and a green cherry).

Another crowd-pleasing ice cream creation was the banana split, a melding of bananas and a scoop each of vanilla, chocolate and strawberry ice cream. Laid out in a long, boat-like

Ice cream sundaes are a soda fountain staple. Soda jerks embellish them with extravagant sauces and toppings – and often a swirl of whipped cream and a cherry on top.

dish, the ice cream trio was then crowned with three different sauces – chocolate, strawberry and pineapple in the classic configuration. Two cities, Latrobe, Pennsylvania and Wilmington, Ohio, both lay claim to the banana split, which each town insists originated during the first decade of the twentieth century.

Ice Cream on the Restaurant Menu and at Home

By the late nineteenth century, the familiar flavour triumvirate of vanilla, chocolate and strawberry was already in place. (This presentation may have derived from the tri-coloured Neapolitan ice cream first produced in the us in 1890, which in turn was possibly derived from the Italian multi-flavoured formed ice cream *spumoni*.) Meanwhile, inventive cookbook writers and restaurant chefs conjured up a rainbow of ice cream flavours and creations. In Paris in 1798, a little more than a hundred years after café Il Procope debuted, another fashionable spot for feasting on ice cream and other refreshments, Café Tortoni, became all the rage of the Parisian smart set. Balzac, Manet and Rossini were among the celebrities who frequented the place. Tortoni's closed in 1893, but a confection, possibly named after its owner, called Biscuit Tortoni, lived on. Sought-after in the us at the turn of the twentieth century, it was composed of a mousse-like frozen cream enriched with crumbled crushed macaroons.

The Neapolitan slice, striped in chocolate, vanilla and strawberry bands, was popular among turn of the 20th-century Americans.

'John Bull', a caricature of a stout, middle-class Englishman, and his family enjoy ices at the famed Café Tortoni, Paris, 1820.

In the US, Charles Ranhofer, the chef of New York's legendary Delmonico's restaurant, was said to have popularized Baked Alaska, the elaborately constructed ice cream dessert composed of sponge cake, ice cream and baked meringue. An array of ice cream flavours – chocolate, cinnamon, ginger, peach, pistachio, tea and pumpernickel bread among them – also graced his 1894 compilation, *The Epicurean*.

Home cooks mastered ice cream making as well. The ingredients for producing ice cream were becoming cheaper. By the second half of the nineteenth century, sugar was becoming affordable. And though at home some cooks still churned ice cream by hand, mechanical ice cream makers were now available. Families could fashion a social occasion out of ice cream making, each family member turning the crank. Now, not only was ice cream becoming quicker and easier to create, but it also doubled as a fun family activity.

American cookbook writer Fannie Merritt Farmer featured more than two dozen recipes for ice cream and other

A modern variation of Baked Alaska made with choux pastry instead of the traditional sponge.

frozen desserts in her *Boston Cooking-School Cook Book* (1896) in flavours ranging from vanilla to ginger. Harking back to the earliest days of ice cream cookery, when ice cream was touted for its health effects, Farmer endorsed ice cream's nutritional value, anointing it the perfect sick room nostrum.

Soda Fountains: A Pop Culture Icon

It wasn't just ordinary citizens who clamoured for ice cream soda fountain treats. They stirred passions among Hollywood stars, as well. Gossip columnists chronicled several screen idols' enthusiasm for ice cream. One who couldn't resist its allure was Swedish film star Ingrid Bergman. 'Like so many others, Ingrid quickly turned into a cherry sundae addict', the *Washington Post* reported in 1940, adding that film studio executives were voicing alarm over the actress's expanding waistline.

Jeanette MacDonald, a 1930s and '40s Hollywood star, is shown eating ice cream on the cover of *Screen Fun* magazine. Soda fountains were frequent backdrops in American movies of the period.

And as soda fountains proliferated, movie directors seized upon the community ice cream eateries as iconic American institutions. Fountains were often tapped to play supporting roles in Broadway plays and in Hollywood films of the 1930s, '40s and '50s. They were the places where small town life and values were enshrined. In Thornton Wilder's 1938 play *Our Town*, for example, Emily Webb and George Gibbs discuss love over an ice cream soda at the drugstore soda fountain in fictional Grover's Corner, New Hampshire. The 1948 MGM musical *A Date with Judy* portrays the romantic yearnings of young girl, Judy, who comes around to Pop's soda fountain, where she meets Pop's handsome nephew. Twenty years later, rival street gangs in *West Side Story*, the 1959 Broadway play about gang warfare in the slums of New York, meet at the neighbourhood drugstore soda fountain where Doc the druggist attempts to broker peace between the warring groups of teens.

And because soda fountains treats are recognized around the world, artists and sculptures have turned to them as themes in their artwork. For example, sculptor Claes Oldenburg's *The Pastry Case: Baked Potato, Sundae, Banana – transformed by Eating* (1965) features four hot fudge sundaes – lined up on a shelf, arrayed in varying states of being devoured.

5
Cones and
Novel Ice Cream Treats

I had always thought that once you grew up you could
do anything you wanted – stay up all night or eat ice
cream straight from the container.
Bill Bryson, American writer

In a 1968 article, *New Yorker* writer L. Rust Hills famously
described a series of intricate manoeuvres for successfully
wrestling a melting ice cream cone into submission. If the
eater revolved 'the cone through the full three hundred
and sixty degrees snapping at the loose gobs of ice cream'
and carried out dozens of other machinations, then the cone
would eventually surrender. In fact, Hills promised, it would
be transformed from its 'unnatural, abhorrent, irregular, cha-
otic form' into an 'ordered, ideal shape that might be envied
by Praxiteles or even Euclid'.

That Hill should devote an entire magazine article to
describing the art and science of licking an ice cream cone
testifies to its enormous popularity the world over. From
Indianapolis to Istanbul, from Chicago to Shanghai, people
turn to cones as hot weather balms. In Italy, with its noble
ice cream traditions, cones are topped with gelato. In India,
Amul, a major Indian dairy company, markets the 'tricone',

a cone enrobed in a coating of nuts and chocolate. It's a type of pre-packaged treat that can be found in freezer compartments the world over. Though national variations abound – in England, for example, a classic combination is the '99', a scoop of soft ice cream in a cone that's paired with a milk chocolate Cadbury Flake or stick of chocolate – the ice cream cone remains remarkably similar from one country to the next. Testifying to the cone's iconic status is the fact that artists worldwide have incorporated images of the beloved frozen street food into their works. Pablo Picasso with *Man With a Straw Hat and an Ice Cream Cone* (1938), Andy Warhol with *Ice Cream Dessert* (*c.* 1950) and Wayne Thiebaud with *Dark Cones* (1964) are just a few of the renowned artists who have celebrated the cone in paintings and sculptures.

A melting mess, England, 2003: a wad of napkins is an essential accessory for eating an ice cream cone.

Even famous artists like Pablo Picasso couldn't resist the allure of ice cream. Here, Picasso features one in his 1937 painting *Man With a Straw Hat and an Ice Cream Cone*.

What accounts for the potent allure of cones, and of their first cousins, ice cream novelties, such as chocolate-covered bars on sticks and popsicles, or lollies, made from water ices? For one, unlike the ice cream sold by hokey pokey vendors, which required the eater to return the container to the seller, ice cream cones and novelties are meant to be eaten on the go. In fact, in the case of the ice cream cone, the eater actually munches on the container, along with the ice cream it holds. It takes about fifty licks to polish off a single scoop of ice cream nestling in a cone – and just a few bites to gobble down its cakey container.

The Cone Comes to the Fair

Though it took a World's Fair in the city of St Louis, Missouri in 1904 to launch the cone as we know it today, the actual cone itself – a wafer that's rolled and baked hard – can trace its lineage all the way back to the Greeks and Romans. Crafted in medieval and Renaissance France and England, wafers were being produced in France as early as the thirteenth century. Baked in special irons, wafers were rolled on wooden pins into cylinder shapes, while others were formed into cornucopias, or cones. Recipes contained flour and milk or water, but could become even more elaborate. One cookbook published in London in 1658, *Archimagirus Anglo-Gallicus; Or, Excellent & Approved Receipts and Experiments in Cookery*, describes a wafer made from a mixture of rosewater, egg whites, flour, sugar and salt. Eighteenth-century English confectioner Frederick Nutt concocted wafers laced with bergamot, an orange scent also used to flavour Earl Grey Tea, as well as with lemon, violet and peppermint. Cones were also faddish embellishments for puddings, bombes and other stylish desserts. For example, Queen Victoria's chef Charles Elmé Francatelli decked out his pudding creations with a festive array of small cones.

How did the cone leap from dessert embellishment to freestanding ice cream treat? No one knows for sure when the first ice cream cone made its debut. But some insist the French were the ones who came up with the idea. British culinary historian Robin Weir points to an 1807 illustration of a young Parisian lady feasting on what appears to be an ice cream cone as offering convincing proof that France was the sweet's true birthplace – a full century before vendors thought to link the two foods at the 1904 St Louis World's Fair.

Others point to English cookbook writer and cooking teacher Agnes B. Marshall, author of *Mrs A. B. Marshall's Cookery Book* (1888) and *Fancy Ices* (1894), as the mother of the ice cream cone. Marshall's recipe for ice cream in baked 'coronets' called for a wafer mixture of flour, eggs, ground almonds and orange water. Marshall wrote: 'These coronets can also be filled with any cream or water ice or set custard or fruits, and served for a dinner, luncheon, or supper dish.' Indeed, Marshall's coronet bore little resemblance to the modern ice cream cone, intended to be savoured while strolling down the street on a hot summer's day. Instead, Marshall's readers were told to dine on her coronet in the customary way – with a set of utensils.

In any event, it took the 1904 World's Fair to provide the spawning ground for the ice cream cone as we now know it. A sensation in its time, the St Louis fair attracted thousands of visitors, and those fairgoers craved walking-around foods. At the event, ice cream sellers and waffle vendors each hawked their wares. Somehow, the idea occurred to one or more of these merchants to unite the two popular snacks into a single delicious treat – the ice cream cone. A few years earlier, Italo Marchiony, an Italian immigrant pushcart vendor from New York, had come up with the idea for a cup-like ice cream cone, which he patented in 1903. Also at about that time, Antonio Valvona of Manchester, England, received a patent for his edible ice cream cup. But it was the vendors at the St Louis fair who popularized the rolled waffle-and-ice cream sensation that would soon take the world by storm.

It's perhaps not surprising that the fair provided a proving ground for the ice cream cone. Scores of vendors were said to have sold ice cream at the event; a number of stands offered waffles as well. So which particular vendor actually came up with the idea for the ice cream cone? As with so many other ice cream 'inventions' and 'firsts', no one knows for sure. One version gives the nod to Syrian immigrant Ernest Hamwi, who ran a booth hawking *zalabia*, a crisp waffle eaten in parts of the Middle East. When Hamwi spotted a nearby ice cream stand, he came up with the idea of filling his waffles with the icy confection and selling it to fairgoers. Yet over the years, others have emerged to challenge Hamwi's claim to being the first to marry a ball of ice cream with a cornucopia-shaped cone. Among them was Lebanese immigrant Abe Doumar who insisted that it was he, and not Hamwi, who had suggested the idea of pairing ice cream with a waffle. Then there was Nick Kabbaz, another Syrian immigrant working the fair. He claimed that he and his brother Albert gave Hamwi the idea for the new confection. Turkish immigrant David Avayou, who also worked at the St Louis fairgrounds, was yet another claimant, and Frank and Charles Menches of Canton, Ohio, who were also involved in peddling food at the event, argued that they were the cone's true originators. In 1952 the International Association of Ice Cream Manufacturers evaluated various ice cream cone invention claims and decided to anoint Hamwi the cone's

Ernest Hamwi was one of several ice cream vendors at the 1904 St Louis World's Fair who claimed to have invented the ice cream cone.

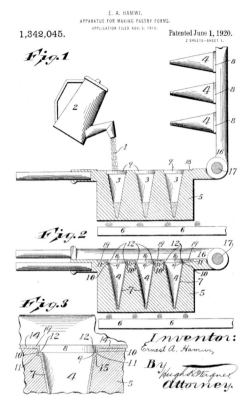

E. A. HAMWI.
APPARATUS FOR MAKING PASTRY FORMS.
APPLICATION FILED NOV. 5, 1918.

1,342,045.

Patented June 1, 1920.
2 SHEETS—SHEET 1.

Fig.1

Fig.2

Fig.3

Inventor:
Ernest A. Hamwi,
By
Hugh K. Wagner
Attorney.

creator. Despite this official designation, disputes still occasionally erupt over who should be awarded the title of ice cream cone 'inventor'.

After the fair ended, Hamwi travelled around the country promoting the new 'coronet'. With a partner, he launched the Cornucopia Waffle Company, which in 1910 became the Missouri Cone Company. It wasn't long before the coronet became known as the cone. The new creation was an instant hit. In fact, cone manufacturers could barely keep up with Americans' seemingly insatiable appetite for the new snack sensation. The

Pacific Coast Cone Company told the *Los Angeles Times* that it was turning out 55 million cones a year – and that it would take a million gallons of ice cream to fill them!

Meanwhile, producers unveiled different cone variations. The crunchy waffle cone, rolled, then baked until it was crisp and rigid, was sold alongside the newer, spongier cake cone, made from batter that was poured into a mould and then baked.

But the cone wasn't the only source of ice cream inventiveness around the turn of the century. Ice cream itself was about to experience a makeover. Fifteen years after the ice cream cone made its debut at the St Louis fair, the Kohr brothers whipped up a batch of an entirely new type of frozen dessert – frozen custard. On the very first weekend that Archie and Elton offered the new treat at their Coney Island, Brooklyn stand, they were wildly successful. They managed to sell eager ice cream lovers more than 18,000 cones of their new, soft ice cream at a nickel a piece. How was this novel frozen confection made? Key to the brother's success was an ice cream freezer that squeezed out a continuous flow of an eggs, cream and sugar mixture that, when it emerged from the machine, filled a cone with a swirl of soft, creamy ice cream.

But the Kohr brothers weren't the only ones wringing profits out of the ice cream cone craze. Whether at the beach or at the amusement park, ice cream cones proved enormously popular. (Ice cream sandwiches – ice cream is 'sandwiched' between two wafers or cookies – debuted around the turn of the twentieth century as summertime street foods.) Costing about a nickel, vendors sold cones to those searching for an affordable escape from the workaday world. Movie palaces offered cones as inducements to get customers to buy tickets to matinees. Cones showed up at Fourth of July picnics.

Hollywood movie directors brandished ice cream cones in front of reluctant actors – in one case a pack of mules employed as movie extras – to gain their cooperation in front of the camera. Everyone, it seemed, loved ice cream cones. 'The ice cream cone booth was the favorite' on a summertime excursion boat trolling Lake Michigan, the *Chicago Daily Tribune* reported in August 1909, adding that fans were lining up for the treat 'from the time the boat started until it got back, mouths full, faces and hands smeared, and clothes covered with the drippings'.

Cones Fuel Ice Cream Industry Growth

In fact so cone-crazy were Americans that they were estimated to have consumed 245 million ice cream cones just two decades after they first appeared at the St Louis fair. Meanwhile, the cone fad helped fuel overall US ice cream consumption. In 1900 annual consumption per capita was about a quart (950 ml). By 1915, that figure had quadrupled, according to the International Association of Ice Cream Vendors. By 1929, the year of the stock market crash, Americans were downing 365 million gallons (1.38 billion litres) of ice cream a year, up from 280 million gallons in 1916.

And the ice cream cone was widely acknowledged to be the engine propelling the ice cream industry's meteoric growth. According to Walter W. Fisk, a Cornell University dairy professor, 'the years from 1900 to 1910' were 'epoch making' when it came to the ice cream trade. 'The cone sold many a gallon of ice cream and made many a dollar for those engaged in the business', he concluded.

Not surprisingly, ice cream cone production soared. At first, cones were produced by hand, but by 1909, an automatic cone roller came on line, and by the 1920s the process was fully mechanized. Batter was dispensed into a cone-shaped mould to form the finished product, which was then baked until crisp. This process allowed the production of hundreds of cones at a time. In 1913 the *New York Times* reported: 'The factories run night and day and more are being built.'

But mushrooming cone production came with a stiff price. Newspapers wrote that cones tainted with boric acid and other contaminants were imperilling ice cream cone eaters, and the press reported lurid tales of children and adults taken ill or even dying after ingesting one of the unsanitary products. Muckraking newspaper writers took off after the cone makers: 'The gelid sweetness which it contains is but a deceptive lure to destruction, for it swarms with germs and is not free from ptomaines, to say nothing of a substantial ingredient of plain filth', warned the *Oregonian* in an August 1910 editorial emblazoned with the headline 'A Conical Evil'. In 1910 government officials accused a group of US producers of infecting their cones with boric acid. (The cone makers responded that the ingredient was needed to stiffen the product so it would retain its shape.) Federal officials wound up confiscating millions of affected cones, including 4.5 million in New York alone, and prosecuted some cone makers as well.

Despite the health scares, the cone's popularity continued to spiral upward. By the time of the Great Depression, the ice cream cone had already established itself as an American icon. Even with the economic downturn, in 1931 Americans dug into their wallets to purchase 300 million of the snacks. Meanwhile, merchants ran promotions – one Georgia purveyor boasted he could balance seven scoops on a single cone – to boost sales. Cones provided employment for many cash-strapped teens, as well. During the 1930s, my mother worked an after-school job at the Kresge drugstore soda fountain in Lynbrook, New York. She and her friend were assigned to stand behind the marble counter and scoop ice cream for cones. Her favourite flavour was chocolate – and she didn't stint when it came to treating herself and her pal to a more-than-occasional-taste. 'We would sit at the counter and make cones', my mother recalled, chuckling. 'One for the customers, one for us.'

Novelties

While cone sales were taking the US by storm, a new group of ice cream entrepreneurs came up with – or in some cases stumbled upon – additional groundbreaking concepts for portable ice cream treats.

Unlike fountain treats or even ice cream cones, all of which required a confectioner or soda jerk to assemble the treat by hand before it could be eaten, novelties arrived from the factory already formed, packaged and ready to be stored in a shop's ice cream freezer. The advent of mechanically refrigerated ice cream cabinets helped fuel the trend, and around 1920, the first automatic ice cream packaging machine rolled off the assembly line. Manufacturers also standardized ice cream mixes. They added corn sugars as well as artificial additives like gum stabilizers to create smoother textures. Carl von Linde, a German engineer, invented mechanical refrigeration in 1870. In 1888 the first refrigerated railway car distributed ice cream throughout the US. In 1929 American Clarence Vogt received a patent for the continuous process freezer. The machine reduced the amount of time it took for ice cream to be manufactured. Better homogenization and pasteurizing techniques were adopted. And beginning in 1925, US states enacted laws setting bacteria standards for commercial ice cream. Also in that year, the first mechanically refrigerated ice cream truck was unveiled at a US dairy show.

Leveraging these advances into broadly embraced ice cream novelty franchises in the second decade of the twentieth century were three go-getter ice cream entrepreneurs: Christian Kent Nelson, creator of the Eskimo Pie; Harry B. Burt Sr, developer of the Good Humor bar; and Frank Epperson, who came up with the idea for the popsicle, a frozen ice on a stick.

Eskimo Pie

Originally dubbed the I-Scream-Bar, Eskimo Pies vaulted to culinary stardom almost immediately following their invention in 1922. In fact, so widely embraced was the new treat that American novelist John Dos Passos could easily incorporate a reference to the Eskimo Pie in a review that appeared in the same year as the product's launch. Why did Americans spurn the works of avant-garde poets like ee cummings, while at the same time appearing eager to embrace exotic new foods like the Eskimo Pie, an 'experiment of surrounding ice-cream with a layer of chocolate', Dos Passos asked.

How did this iconic snack get its start? School teacher and ice cream shop owner Christian Nelson came up with the idea for the treat – a block of vanilla ice cream is enrobed in a milk chocolate candy coating – when a customer couldn't decide whether to purchase ice cream or a chocolate candy bar. Nelson then teamed for a time with Russell Stover (later founder of the eponymous candy company), and it was Stover who came up with the name 'Eskimo Pie'. The chocolate covered bar received a patent (later rescinded on the grounds that there was nothing new about dipping ice cream in a coating) in 1922.

To make Eskimo Pies, a hot chocolate coating heated to 115°F (46°C) was applied to the ice cream. But instead of the steamy chocolate melting the ice cream, the frozen ice cream actually caused the chocolate to harden. The bars were then wrapped in aluminum foil – another new invention.

To expand the business, Nelson licensed independent dairies and producers to manufacture the bars, but they could barely keep up with demand. One licensee, the Huber Ice Cream Company of Bridgeport, Connecticut, reported that it was shipping up to 3,000 dozen Eskimo Pies a day to the New York area alone. US grocery chains, like A&P, Safeway and Piggly Wiggly, began stocking the new sensation as well.

The square bars, with their trademark wrappers sporting a midnight sun, played starring roles at county fairs, barn dances, special matinee Christmas performances for orphans, and at other community events and celebrations. It was said that during the 1920s, the Eskimo Pie company single-handedly supported the world cocoa market. Soda fountains stocked them. And distributors around the country heavily promoted the new treat. In an ad touting the Eskimo Pie, an Atlanta manufacturer urged buyers to sidle up to the soda fountain counter, 'slap a nickel on the marble, and demand of the soda jerker, "Gimme a George Mason Eskimo Pie!"'

Despite the Eskimo Pie's success, Nelson never got rich from his invention. Licensees didn't always pay up and by 1924 he had sold Eskimo Pies to R. S. Reynolds, the aluminium manufacturer; Nelson worked there until he retired in 1961. Today, the Eskimo Pie Ice Cream brand is owned by Swiss multinational Nestlé.

Almost immediately after their invention in 1922, Eskimo Pies (or in the UK, 'choc ices') achieved dessert snack stardom. Each chocolate-covered brick was wrapped in aluminum foil, a newfangled invention at the time.

Ice Cream Promotes Good Humor

It took one small but important step to transform the Eskimo Pie into an even more iconic frozen treat – the ice cream bar on a stick. The idea originated with Harry B. Burt, Jr, a candy and ice cream maker from Youngstown, Ohio. Inspired by Nelson's success with the Eskimo Pie, Burt decided to fashion his own chocolate-covered ice cream bar. But eating it proved to be exceedingly messy. So an ingenious solution was devised: insert a stick into the bar to keep the chocolate and ice cream from melting all over eaters' hands. Thus was born one of the most enduring ice cream novelties ever invented – the ice cream on a stick, or 'sucker' as it was first known. Burt received a patent for his creation in 1923, but to secure it he had to deliver a bribe – a pail chock full of the frozen treats – to US patent office officials in Washington, DC.

The name 'Good Humor' was derived from the belief at the time that a person's 'humour', or temperament, was related to the humour of the palate, or sense of taste. Through the years, the company touted the benefits of eating a 'Good Humor'. 'Ice cream is America's daily dish of delight – the original joy food', proclaimed a July 1931 ad in the *Los Angeles Times*. 'I've never yet seen anyone eating it that wasn't in a good humor', the ad promised the newspaper's readers. Ice cream fans quickly picked up on the marketing message. A local golfer reported to the *Atlanta Constitution* in 1936: 'I have had to have about two a day in order to keep a "good humor" after my bad rounds, and the name "good humor" seems to help.'

Vans and Trucks

For many ice cream lovers, especially in the US and Britain, nothing evokes the carefree days of childhood like the tingling of an ice cream van's bells. In Britain, for example, the strains of 'Greensleeves' kindle memories of summer days spent racing after colourful Mr Whippy ice cream vans, those beloved motorized purveyors of ice cream bars on a stick and other frozen treats that began patrolling British villages and towns in the 1950s. In the US, the mere recollection of Good Humor's square, white ice cream trucks ignites the same kind of nostalgic response from ice cream lovers of a certain age. In fact, so embedded in American culture are

Good Humor trucks and their friendly white-uniformed drivers that the duo turn up frequently in movie scripts – from *God's Little Acre* (1958) in which Buddy Hackett plays Pluto Swint, an ice cream truck driver, to *Borat: Cultural Learnings of America for Make Benefit Glorious Nation of Kazakhstan* (2006), in which Sacha Baron Cohen embarks on a trip across America in an ice cream truck.

The idea of peddling ice cream on the street was, of course, nothing new. Hokey pokey vendors had pioneered it. But Burt took the concept a critical step further. He harnessed new refrigeration technology to deliver frozen snacks – there were vanilla bars covered in a chocolate coating and ones swathed in shredded coconut – nationwide in trucks with freezer compartments to keep the goods cold and frosty. Initially, Burt launched a fleet of a dozen trucks in the Midwestern city of Youngstown, Ohio. Fitted out with bells and driven by men outfitted in snappy white uniforms and crisp caps, Good Humor projected unalloyed wholesomeness. Perhaps with the cone poisoning scandals fresh in its mind, the company trumpeted its image of purity. In one 1930s ad, the ice cream firm boasted that 'Good Humor's purity never is sullied by careless hands, unclean air, sloppy packing. Good Humor always comes clean.'

The sparkling white trucks and their inexpensive frozen snacks proved to be a huge hit. Headquartered in Brooklyn, New York, Good Humor installed production plants in Chicago, Detroit, Boston, Newark, Hartford and elsewhere to satisfy growing demand. Kids loved the treats on a stick. Adults did too. Housewives received booklets filled with recipes for ice cream creations based on the company's brands for those times when 'milady's luncheon or dinner goes festive'. One suggestion – touted as elegant *and* economical – paired angel food cake with one of Good Humor's fourteen

The Good Humor ice cream man delighted mid-20th-century American children with his square white truck full of frozen treats, 1942.

flavours of ice cream for a dish, the company insisted, that would cost the hostess only $3 for 12 servings.

Even movie moguls apparently loved Good Humor. According to one possibly apocryphal tale, the head of Columbia movie studios, Harry Cohen, is said to have been in the midst of an argument with his brother, Jack. When Cohen heard an ice cream truck's bell ringing as it drove down the street near his office, he stopped fighting, took orders, ran to the window, and called down the order: 'One chocolate! Two strawberry!' before going back to fighting with his brother.

Meanwhile, in England, mobile ice cream sellers also hit the road – but they drove tricycles, not motorized vans. (Ice cream bikes survive to this day in places like Luang Prubang, Laos, where pedalling ice cream vendors dish up cones of coconut or strawberry to children and adults alike.) In England, sausage maker Thomas Wall, in an effort to offset slow summer sales, decided to produce ice cream. Around 1923, Wall's launched the first fleet of ice cream bicycles in London. Armed with the slogan 'Stop Me and Buy One', the company's sales mushroomed, garnering £13,719 by 1924. According to the London Canal Museum, which is housed in the building in which ice cream merchant Carlo Gatti conducted his ice-importing business, Wall's then ordered fifty new tricycles and fitted them with freezer compartments on the front; by 1927 Wall's was earning £444,000 a year from its ice cream sales.

Ice cream wasn't the only frozen treat to find itself impaled on a wooden stick. Water ices received similar treatment. In 1905 a young boy named Frank Epperson accidentally left some flavoured water and a stirring stick on his front porch one winter day. The mixture froze, and Epperson would occasionally make the 'Eppsicle' for his friends. The true launch of the product, however, didn't come until 1923. In that year, the inventor was running a lemonade stand in Oakland when he realized the commercial potential of his frozen ice on a stick. He renamed it the Popsicle. Today, the Popsicle brand is a division of Anglo-Dutch multinational, Unilever. Popsicles or ice pops, as they're called in the US, and ice lollies, as they're known in England, India and elsewhere, are beloved refreshments on hot summer days.

6

Ice Cream Goes Mass Market

I doubt whether the world holds for anyone a more soul-stirring
surprise than the first adventure with ice-cream.
Heywood Broun, American journalist

Americans' can-do spirit helped transform ice cream from an
occasional and expensive delicacy into an affordable everyday food. But there were other factors at work as well. The
price of sugar declined, as did the cost of other ingredients
like cream and eggs. But it took more than sugar and cream
to create a thriving ice cream industry. It also required a
supply of refrigerants – one that wasn't tied to the vagaries
of the weather.

You Don't Need a Weatherman

By the time of the First World War, the natural ice business
was in a state of decline. Setbacks – many due to fickle winter
weather – plagued the industry. In fact, a major problem hob-
bling the natural ice business was its dependence on reliably
cold winters in the world's ice-producing regions, such as
New England in the US and Norway in Europe. Ice, of course,

melts. All it took was a protracted winter warm spell, and the supply of ice simply vanished. During the unseasonably temperate winter of 1860, for example, the Hudson River in New York failed to produce a single usable ice crop. And with factories and mills throwing off ever greater amounts of pollutants, unsullied waterways were becoming scarce.

With ice cream's growing popularity, the need for ice escalated. In fact, to make, store and ship 100 gallons (379 litres) of ice cream required vast quantities of ice: nearly a ton, according to an estimate provided by Cornell University dairy professor Walter W. Fisk in his 1919 *The Book of Ice Cream*. All together, Fisk estimated, churning ice cream required 614 lb of ice. Hardening and storing it demanded another 914 lb. And an additional 400 lb were needed to ship and deliver it, and to ice cabinets for storing it.

It was only a matter of time before artificial ice – its greatest selling point was its reliability – displaced fickle natural ice. For centuries efforts had been underway to perfect artificial ice. During the American Civil War, artificial ice made important strides. The North blockaded the Southern states. That meant that the South was forced to find another way to refrigerate foods. In the closing years of the war, New Orleans became a centre of artificial ice production, according to a 1922 account in the trade magazine *Soda Fountain*. By the 1880s, artificial refrigeration was being installed in breweries, and the 1893 World's Columbian Exposition in Chicago featured a large refrigeration unit. Europeans were slow to adopt the new chilling process, but in the US, beginning at the end of the nineteenth century, artificial ice overtook natural ice as the refrigerant of choice. By 1920, the same period during which gas and electric refrigerators were starting to supplant ice boxes in US kitchens, the number of ice factories had jumped to 2,867 from just a handful in the

Fussell-Young Ice Cream Company trucks, probably Washington, DC, between 1921 and 1922.

1870s, according to a 1922 survey in *Soda Fountain* magazine. Artificial ice was clearly overtaking natural ice. '[U]nofficial estimates by accepted authorities indicate that the quantity obtained from natural sources has steadily decreased coincidentally with the big increase in artificial production,' concluded the journal.

Ice Cream Goes to War

By the turn of the twentieth century, advances in refrigeration and other technologies were spurring growth and consolidation in the ice cream industry. In England, for example, food company J. Lyons & Co., which began operations in 1894 as a chain of teashops, soon morphed into a major food wholesaling and retailing concern, manufacturing and shipping ice cream and other convenience foods all over Great Britain. The early British ice cream industry owed much of its success to American ice cream manufacturing methods. In fact, Lyons' owners studied us food manufacturing processes and adopted them to produce foods for UK consumers, such as the ice cream 'brick'. By 1939, Lyons was turning out 3.5 million gallons (16 million litres) of ice cream a year.

In the US, meanwhile, ice cream companies were consolidating. In 1926, for instance, Breyers became a division of the National Dairy Products Corporation (NDPC). But the Depression arrived to put a crimp in ice cream sales worldwide. With the outbreak of the Second World War, ice cream production was severely curtailed in both the US and Great Britain; in England, manufacturing of ice cream was banned outright. But the war also endowed ice cream with a new-found purpose. Wall's tricycles were enlisted by the British military to serve the war effort. And US battlefield planners exploited ice cream's power as a morale booster for the troops fighting overseas. So critical was ice cream thought to be in shoring up servicemen's spirits that a miniature ice cream factory was constructed in the South Pacific to provide ice cream to the troops. Weighing 1,200 lb (544 kg), the plant was able to operate in 120-degree temperatures and crank out batches of ice cream in seven to fourteen minutes, according to press accounts at the time. The US Navy also built a floating ice cream parlour. Built at a cost of more than $1 million, its crew could pump out 1,500 gallons (5,678 litres) of ice cream an hour.

Ice cream was also enlisted to soothe the temperament, if not heal the wounds, of American soldiers recovering stateside from battlefield injuries. 'They can't get enough of it,' a

Navy dietitian stationed in a Staten Island, New York hospital told the *New York Times* in December 1943. 'And the flavor doesn't matter, just as long as it's ice cream.'

On the home front in the US, ingredients like vanilla, chocolate and coffee were in short supply. Schrafft's, the beloved string of eateries, discontinued the sale of ice cream by the pound, while American newspaper food writers tried to help their readers cope with shortages. Throughout the 1930s and '40s, newspaper food writers – Clementine Paddleford, Dorothea Duncan and Marian Manners all wrote widely read columns – were urging homemakers to serve ice cream treats to party guests. In a 1935 *Washington Post* column titled 'Sundae Takes High Position as Dessert', Dorothea Duncan stated that 'the combination will always be a favorite where Americans are concerned.' Some concoctions incorporated everyday foods that were reimagined into entirely new taste sensations. Manners, for example, penned a recipe for a 'corn crispy sundae' in which finely crushed corn flakes were sprinkled over the ice cream.

But when the war came along, food writers cautioned that rationing would place limits on ice cream cookery. Paddleford urged readers in a July 1944 *Los Angeles Times* column to scrimp on ice cream by layering it with fruit or to supplement it with a serving of sherbet. Wartime rationing also threatened the existence of the beloved ice cream cone. Cone manufacturers couldn't get wheat flour, so several Philadelphia companies improvised, concocting cones out of crushed, sweetened popcorn.

Surprisingly, ice cream could sometimes find itself the unwitting victim of bouts of wartime hysteria. In the summer of 1940, for example, the *New York Times* reported that the FBI had launched an investigation into a 'mysterious G signal' that a neighbour had reportedly seen hanging on the window of the suburban Westchester, New York home of a German Embassy official. As it turned out, the suspicious sign was not a secret code for some nefarious Nazi plot, but rather the ambassador's effort to signal the local Good Humor man to deliver ice cream to his house.

The Post-War Years

In England ice cream rationing continued until 1953. Even when food restrictions were finally lifted, producers there continued to make ice cream from vegetable fat and milk powder and not cream. Still, the end of the war proved a boon to the sales of ice cream. In October 1947, according to the London Canal Museum, Wall's sold 3,300 of its tricycles and invested in freezers for shops, speeding the distribution of the treat throughout Great Britain.

In the US, with the return of peacetime, Americans re-sumed their passionate love affair with ice cream. In fact, in 1946 annual US consumption per capita reached an historic high of 23 lb (10.4 kg) per person, the US Department of Agriculture reported. Why the spike in sales? For one, there was pent up demand driven by wartime restrictions. For another, Second World War veterans were returning home, moving to the suburbs and producing bumper crops of children. The baby boom was in full swing, unleashing a mammoth national appetite for ice cream. Eating snacks between meals also fuelled the desire for foods to nibble on, and ice cream fitted the bill, especially in the warm summer months. To satisfy the escalating demand, the commercial ice cream industry swung into high gear, basing 'its hopes for the future on a statistical fact – more babies are being born today than ever before', as a July 1954 *Nation's Business* story, 'Ice Cream

Cones Scoop Up 24,000,000 Sales', put it. And ice cream was squarely within the financial reach of most American consumers. 'Ice-cream cones and soft drinks have become essentials even for the poorest city family with children', wrote the *Christian Science Monitor* in 1948.

Given the explosion in the number of ice cream devotees, it wasn't surprising that by 1950 US ice cream consumption had soared, reaching a staggering 537 million gallons (2.03 billion litres). To churn out all that frozen goodness, the industry employed 80,000 workers, according to industry statistics. In the post-war period, British ice cream consumption rose as well. Lyons expanded its share of the market, acquiring smaller players, such as Eldorado, Neilson's, Midland Counties, Walkers Dairies, Tonnibel and Bertorelli. (During the 1950s a young scientist named Margaret Roberts worked as a food researcher for J. Lyons & Co.; Margaret Roberts Thatcher later became Britain's prime minister.)

Other emerging post-war trends signalled enormous shifts in the way ice cream was marketed and sold. When the troops came home in 1945, most people still bought ice cream outside the home from soda fountains, ice cream parlours and confectioners. In 1946 the US War Production Board placed the estimate of the number of soda fountains in the United States at 120,000, but with the advent of fast food chains in the 1950s, that number would soon start to tumble.

The Good Humor Man as Neighbourhood Hero

Indeed, times were changing. After the war, the Good Humor man became a fixture in US suburban neighbourhoods. Kids swarmed the trucks, buying treats on a stick. Actor and comedian Eddie Murphy recalled in one of his sketches the powerful allure of the ice cream truck that patrolled his Long Island, New York neighbourhood.

By 1951 packaged ice cream was accounting for almost a third of US ice cream sales. Housewives could now whip a container of ice cream out of their home freezers. No trip to the ice cream parlour was required. Beginning in the early 1960s, other snack foods – so-called fast food, sold from automobile-friendly roadside stands – began to supplant both the iconic corner drugstore soda fountain and eventually, in 1976, the familiar Good Humor truck. America's infatuation with the automobile – you could hop in your car and speed off to the local hamburger stand for a quick bite – was in full bloom. Then, there was the convenience of plucking a half-gallon of pre-packaged ice cream – now filled with air and emulsifiers and stabilizers to prolong its shelf life – from your supermarket's freezer case.

The Mix Gets Emulsified

The composition of ice cream itself was also changing. Merchandizing ice cream in supermarkets required that the product sit on the shelf for long periods of time. That meant finding additives to keep it smooth and tasty and to prevent nagging ice crystals from forming. Ice cream mixes of yore – simple amalgams of cream, sugar and flavourings – were out. Emulsifiers and stabilizers to create a velvety product were in. Commercial ice cream makers, like Sealtest, Bordens and Breyers, radically changed the ingredients that went into ice cream mixes. Standard components now included non-fat dry milk, skimmed milk and whole milk; cane or beet sugar, or corn syrup; artificial flavourings; and emulsifiers and

The process of making ice cream.

stabilizers. Manufacturers also boosted the amount of air (called 'overrun' in industry jargon) in commercial products. The result? An ice cream that was inexpensive and long-lasting – but one whose texture was much thinner and fluffier than that found in traditional ice creams.

The trend toward industrial ice cream took hold in Great Britain as well, though in other parts of Europe, like Italy and France, durable, indigenous ice cream traditions kept commercial ice cream at bay – at least until the forces of globalization swept US brands into European markets, beginning in the second half of the twentieth century.

Meanwhile, in the US and Great Britain, national rules were put in place that regulated ice cream's composition. In the US federal regulators stipulated that ice cream must contain at least 10 per cent butterfat. In Britain a product could be sold as ice cream if it contained 5 per cent fat and not less than 2.5 per cent milk protein. Ice cream there could also contain non-milk vegetable fats and oils. The amount of air was stipulated as well. In the US the legal overrun limit is 100 per cent, resulting in an ice cream that's about half air. (Premium ice cream contains far less air, helping to achieve its characteristic silky, tense texture. These higher-quality ice creams also contain more fat, around 13 per cent to 15 per cent for premium and 16 per cent to 20 per cent for super-premium.)

Ice cream production at this point was highly mechanized. Producers placed the ingredients into a mixing tank where they were blended together, reported the International Dairy Foods Association. The mixture was pasteurized and homogenized to enhance creaminess. Next it was cooled to about 40°F (4.4°C) and frozen using the continuous freezer method. This froze the ice cream one batch at a time. Air was whipped into the ice cream. Fruits, chocolate chips and other solid flavourings could be added at this stage. Finally, the ice cream was packaged and moved into a hardening room where sub-zero temperatures froze it solid.

Ice Cream Takes to the Road

Meanwhile, the automobile was sparking enormous changes in Americans' ice cream eating habits. Dotting the roadways beginning in the 1930s, ice cream stands proliferated. Some of the earliest stands – many boasted sloping roofs angled suggestively in the direction of an adjacent highway – were mom-and-pop operations situated on secondary roads. The idea was to seduce slow-moving cars to stop by for a cone or cup of ice cream. Little more than hulking cement billboards, mid-century ice cream stands boasted shapes and signage brazenly trumpeting their wares. There were stands in the shape of upside-down ice cream cones. Others were conceived of as igloos and castles. Nearly all were bedecked with gaudy, flashing neon signs. If travelling motorists weren't already sold on the idea that an ice cream cone would offer a fun-filled break from the tedium of the road, then the stands' flamboyant architecture loudly broadcasted that message. (In Louisiana, scores of former ice cream stands have been converted in recent years to drive-through daiquiri shops, perhaps the ultimate expression of roadside dining exuberance.)

Soft Ice Cream Creates a Stir

The stands were just the right type of retail outlet for the post-war ice cream-loving times. Partly aided by these roadside outfits, ice cream cone sales went through the roof. By 1953, 6 billion of the treats were sold in the US, according to industry figures.

To meet the escalating demand, a hundred cone companies poured an estimated 50 million lb (22.7 million kg) of flour and 3.5 million lb of sugar into cone-making machines. And it wasn't just kids who were lapping up cones. Adults loved them, too. In fact, in a bid to attract adult customers, a total of 65 per cent of the cones produced in the early 1950s were of the flat-bottomed variety – said to be more appealing to grown-ups than the more common waffle cone.

With a seemingly insatiable demand emanating from baby boomers and their parents, new ice cream vendors entered

A British ice cream van of the type used since the 1950s.

the market. In the UK Mr Softee and Mr Whippy peddled soft ice cream from vans in English villages and towns, beginning in the late 1950s. In the US the demand for soft-serve ice cream soon eclipsed that of the regular, hard-packed variety. By 1950, Americans were lapping up five times as much soft ice cream as they had three years earlier, while hard ice cream consumption had slipped 16 per cent from its 1947 levels. By 1957 more than 12,000 drive-in stores were dotting the US roadways. And fans were digging into 150 million gallons (568 million litres) of the swirled soft confection annually.

Dairy Queen

It wasn't long before regional and national chains in the US – Tastee Freez, Carvel, Kohr's and Dairy Queen, to name a few – pushed aside many of the original mom and pops. One of the most successful of these new purveyors was Dairy Queen, founded in 1938. From the opening of the first shop in Kankakee, Illinois, the fledgling company – launched by the father and son team of J. F. and H. A. McCulloughs of Green River, Illinois – flourished. In 1946, sales of their soft serve – unlike frozen custard, it was made without eggs – totalled $75,000, according to company figures. By 1950 the company was raking in $35 million from its 1,400 outlets. By the mid-1950s the company was claiming 2,600 shops located throughout the US.

Franchising was the key to Dairy Queen's growth. Starting in the late 1940s, the company had instituted a system in which store owners were granted a specific geographic territory in exchange for paying an upfront fee and royalties. Today, Dairy Queen operates more than 5,900 restaurants in the United States, Canada and twenty foreign countries. (Texas claims boasting rights to the most Dairy Queens, with 600 outlets.) International expansion began in 1953.

Eager customers line up outside a Dairy Queen store.

Dairy Queen now runs stores outside the US in places like Canada, Australia, Japan, the Philippines, Hong Kong and India. Today, Dairy Queen is owned by multinational Berkshire Hathaway.

Howard Johnson and His 28 Flavours

In 'The Oranging of America', a 1976 short story by American writer Max Apple, a fictional Howard Johnson embarks on a road trip across America. Cruising US highways in a limousine fitted out with a back-seat ice cream freezer containing a selection of eighteen ice cream flavours, the restaurant magnate launches a quest to find new locales for his roadside eateries. 'He raised his right arm and its shadow spread across the continent like a prophecy', Apple wrote of his road-tripping restaurateur.

As it turned out, the aspirations of the imaginary Johnson didn't differ substantially from those of the actual man. Howard Johnson introduced Americans to an expanded palette of ice cream flavours. But just as importantly, he cemented a trend that ice cream-stand owners had already begun to exploit – the marriage of ice cream-eating and automobile trips.

In 1925 Howard Dearing Johnson, then a young druggist with a soda fountain in Wollaston, Massachusetts, doubled the fat content in his ice cream; customers flocked to his store for the rich treat. Predicting that Americans were ready to expand beyond the traditional favourites of vanilla and chocolate, Johnson unveiled a line-up of 28 flavours – from maple walnut to banana. Soon he added lunch and snack foods, such as fried clams and hot dogs. An American roadside dining institution was born.

Like the mom-and-pop ice cream-stand operators, Johnson figured out that Americans' infatuation with the automobile, and the lifestyle it spawned, was the key to marketing his product. So Johnson followed the Second World War veterans and their families to the suburbs that were springing up around the nation's cities. There, amongst the split levels and ranch houses, the automobile was king. In fact, in the newly minted towns, residents were totally dependent on their cars for connecting with essential neighbourhood services – from grocery stores to dining establishments.

So Johnson embarked on an expansion plan in which he situated his orange-roofed eateries in burgeoning suburban subdivisions. From Levittown, New York, to Kankakee, Illinois, Howard Johnson restaurants became familiar dining landmarks. Accommodating suburbanites' automobiles was key to the business's success. The Levittown restaurant was typical. It boasted 26,000 square feet (2,415 sq. m) of parking – an area that that dwarfed the size of the eatery itself.

By 1952 Johnson had served more than 200 million diners at his 355 stores. Investors – including Second World War general and US President Dwight D. Eisenhower who became a partner in a Washington, DC HoJos, as the chain was affectionately called – clamoured to buy into the business. By the beginning of the next decade, the number of HoJos in the US had nearly doubled. And when a major highway, the Pennsylvania Turnpike, opened to traffic in 1940, Johnson was given the nod to put the roadway's eateries in place. By 1952 there were twenty-one HoJos on the Pennsylvania artery alone, eleven positioned on the New Jersey Turnpike, and one on the Maine highway. One hundred million Americans a year were taking to US roads by the early 1960s – and Johnson was feeding a good number of them.

For many Americans of a certain age, Howard Johnson's meant a stop along the highway for an ice cream cone. The first Howard Johnson's was built in Wollaston, Massachusetts in 1924 and featured a staggering array of 28 flavours.

This Lynnfield, Massachusetts HoJos, as the chain was affectionately known, was built in 1933. It boasted a substantial parking lot to lure suburban families who flocked to the chain for a meal of fried clams and ice cream.

Soon Johnson's dining empire was equated in the minds of many Americans with the concept of roadside dining. 'In most states east of the Mississippi River, the term "Howard Johnson" has become synonymous with roadside restaurant', the *New York Times* wrote in a September 1952 story chronicling the chain's success. '[A]s long a automobiles continue to pour out of Detroit, Howard Johnson won't worry too much: every car that rolls off the production line has built-in customers', wrote the *Chicago Defender* in 1961, estimating that America's roadside restaurants were pulling in $6 billion of business annually.

Ice cream was HoJo's biggest seller, accounting in 1955 for a quarter of all sales. And it seemed as if the HoJos formula would be easy to export to Europe. But when the company opened its first store in Amsterdam in the 1970s, customers spurned its products. And trouble was brewing at home as well. In the 1960s charges of racism dogged the chain. Several outlets operating in southern states refused to serve African-Americans. In fact, HoJos became embroiled in controversy when in 1961 President John F. Kennedy was forced to issue a personal apology to a Sierra Leone diplomat who had been refused service at a Hagerstown, Maryland store. Soon, nagging cleanliness and food quality issues surfaced – and in a blow to the ice cream's brand, customers complained that some HoJos outlets were carrying fewer than the vaunted 28 flavours. Perhaps the fatal blow was struck when the New Jersey Turnpike authority decided to terminate Howard Johnson's roadside concession contract in 1973.

Today, almost no original Howard Johnson buildings remain; in 2005 the Times Square restaurant in New York was shuttered forever. A year later, La Mancha Group, LLC took control of the food and beverage rights, according to www.HoJoland.com, a Howard Johnson fan site. Meanwhile HoJo devotees keep the flame alive through various Internet sites, hoping for a resurrection of the iconic roadside dining spots.

As for the restaurant magnate himself, Johnson always considered himself an ice cream man at heart. He was said to down a dish a day and to have kept a freezer full in his New York penthouse apartment. Yet despite his epic accomplishments – including the rainbow of 28 flavours – Johnson's attempts to convince Americans to become more adventurous ice cream eaters fell short. At mid-century, fully half of US ice cream fans still preferred vanilla. In fact, Johnson appeared to have died a disappointed man, reported a *New York Times* obituary in 1972. Try as he might, the restaurant chieftain believed that in one key respect, he had failed mightily. 'I spent my whole life developing scores of flavors,' he lamented, 'and yet most people still say, "I'll take vanilla."'

The Premiums

Johnson may have felt that weaning Americans from their passion for vanilla, chocolate and strawberry was a near hopeless cause. But other ice cream innovators would come along who would garner more success from expanding Americans' ice cream tastes.

Two who thought US ice cream fans were ready for more sophisticated offerings were brothers-in-law Burton 'Burt' Baskin and Irvine 'Irv' Robbins. Baskin and Robbins launched their shops – at first the two men operated separate businesses – in the 1940s. In 1945 Robbins opened Snowbird Ice Cream in Glendale, California, while a year later, his brother-in-law started Burton's Ice Cream Shop in nearby Pasadena. In 1953 the two men joined forces to usher in a new era of ice cream inventiveness, a chain that offered up an array of 31 flavours (one for each day of the month). To entice ice cream eaters to come into their shops, they struck a bubble gum vibe, with an aesthetic that portrayed smiling clowns and a riot of brown and pink polka dots. And despite Howard Johnson's fears that Americans would never stray from their preference for plain old vanilla, ice cream devotees flocked to the stores. By the mid-1960s Baskin and Robbins were operating 400 franchises in the US. In the 1970s the company stepped into the global market, unveiling outlets in Japan, Saudi Arabia, Korea and Australia. Today, Baskin-Robbins, with over 3,100 stores in 30 countries, is part of Dunkin' Brands, owner of another global snack icon, Dunkin' Donuts.

Over the years, Baskin-Robbins has rolled out a series of memorable flavours that captured the world's imagination. Who can forget classics like Lunar Cheesecake (honouring Neil Armstrong's 1969 moon landing) or Cocoa a Go-Go, a tribute to the 1980s craze for go-go dancing? During the 2008 US presidential race, Baskin-Robbins introduced Straight Talk Crunch for Republican standard-bearer John McCain, and Whirl of Change for Democratic candidate Barack Obama.

In a 1976 interview in the *New York Times*, Robbins took credit for Americans' newfound delight in offbeat ice cream flavours. 'They're not embarrassed to ask for some of these wild flavors', the bespectacled ice cream man said. 'I think we've had a little bit to do with making it acceptable.'

The Allure of European Sophistication

With their innovative flavours sporting whimsical monikers, Baskin and Robbins presaged the creative genius of later ice

A marketing ploy pays off: Häagen-Dazs played to Americans' desire for a touch of continental class by christening its new ice cream with an entirely fictitious European-sounding name.

cream innovators, especially Ben Cohen and Jerry Greenfield, founders of Ben & Jerry's ice cream.

But first, another pair of ice cream entrepreneurs – Polish immigrant and Bronx resident Reuben Mattus, along with his wife, Rose – tapped into Americans' budding fascination with exotic European foods. During the 1960s and '70s growing numbers of Americans were venturing abroad for vacations. While travelling in Europe they developed a taste for more sophisticated fare. The Mattuses' new ice cream tapped into this newfound worldliness, evoking Old World style, elegance and craftsmanship. And US ice cream lovers were instantly seduced.

In 1959, after years of working in the family's ice cream business, the Mattuses decided to strike out on their own. They had a hunch that ice cream aficionados might be willing to pay more for a product aimed at adults, with a foreign-sounding name that was perceived to be chic and a little luxurious.

Employing a tactic that ranks among the most daring in food marketing history, the Mattuses dubbed their new product 'Häagen-Dazs'. With a foreign-sounding, unpronounceable name that was supposed to evoke Scandinavian elegance, Häagen-Dazs became the dessert choice of stylish diners from coast to coast. To convey additional authenticity, they even affixed an umlaut to the word and, to hit the point home, drew a map of Scandinavia on the new ice cream's carton. Of course, no Scandinavian had ever uttered a word that even remotely resembled Häagen-Dazs. (The ice cream was produced entirely in Teaneck, New Jersey.) Still, the audacious campaign worked. Almost instantly, Häagen-Dazs acquired a considerable cachet. In the 1970s and '80s few stylish hostesses would have neglected to serve Häagen-Dazs coffee ice cream for dessert at a dinner party or special event.

By 1973 Häagen-Dazs, which had begun life as a niche gourmet product, was being sold in supermarkets throughout the US. To boost the brand's allure, the company created an unusually dense, rich mix and touted its use of high-quality natural ingredients, such as vanilla from Madagascar. Initially, the ice cream came in only three flavours – vanilla, chocolate and coffee. By reducing the amount of air and jacking up the percentage of butterfat, Häagen-Dazs was able to imbue its ice cream with a velvety voluptuousness. In fact, Häagen-Dazs had crafted what was to become known as 'super-premium' ice cream, a product enriched with about 16 per cent butterfat (as compared with 10 per cent for regular ice cream), and much less air as filler.

By 1981, according to the *New York Times*, the company had produced about 40 million pints (18.9 million litres), with an estimated $30 million in revenue. By that point there were 70 US Häagen-Dazs franchises, offering up nineteen flavours of the voluptuous, intensely flavoured ice cream.

In 1982 Häagen-Dazs began selling its ice cream abroad in countries ranging from Japan to Germany. When the velvety frozen confection was introduced in Europe, its richness and denseness contrasted with the lower fat varieties that many Europeans were used to. Still, when Häagen-Dazs opened its doors in Paris in 1990, locals clamoured for the new treat. Today Häagen-Dazs has outlets in 54 countries with 850 shops, from Paris to Rio de Janeiro.

These days, the Häagen-Dazs brand is owned worldwide by General Mills. However, in the United States and Canada only, Häagen-Dazs is marketed by Nestlé.

Ben & Jerry's: Funky and Rich

During the period that Howard Johnson was blazing a trail of 28 flavours through America's postwar suburbs, Ben Cohen and Jerry Greenfield were growing up outside New York City in Merrick, Long Island. After college, the two friends reunited and when the start-up costs of their planned bagel business turned out to be too steep, they settled on ice cream instead. To learn the trade, they enrolled in a Penn State University ice cream-making correspondence course.

Soon, Cohen and Greenfield would make ice cream history.

Though it may seem odd that the duo chose Burlington, Vermont for their enterprise, with its long, frigid winters, there were pluses to the unusual locale that included little competition and an endless supply of ravenous, ice cream-loving University of Vermont college students. In the summer of 1978, Cohen and Greenfield opened their first ice cream shop in a renovated gas station. The first two flavours offered were vanilla and Mint Oreo Cookie.

With an initial investment of $12,000, Greenfield and Cohen managed to parlay Ben & Jerry's into a worldwide ice cream phenomenon. It wasn't long before the pair was packing their ice cream in pints and delivering it to stores. By the end of 1988, the two childhood friends were selling $47 million of ice cream a year at 80 shops in eighteen states nationwide.

What accounted for this phenomenal success?

Arguably, the goofy ice cream monikers – from Cherry Garcia to Chunky Monkey – drove as many sales as the rich homemade-style confection itself, which the childhood friends crafted at their Vermont factory. And from the beginning, the company exuded a distinctive 1960s vibe. (The product's packaging sports portraits of the scruffy, bearded company founders looking like they've just stepped out of Woodstock.) In fact, to cement loyalty among ice cream eaters, from the company's earliest years, Ben & Jerry's ran feel-good promotions, like Free Cone Day (when pregnant women got two free ice creams).

Indeed, it was Cohen and Greenfield's dedication to social justice issues that helped burnish the company's reputation. In 1985 the Ben & Jerry's Foundation was established. Over the years, the company has supported social activism campaigns ranging from supporting efforts to halt climate change – 'Take it from a couple of ice cream guys: if it's melted, it's ruined', Ben once said – to children's causes.

But it was the rich, flavourful ice cream that assumed centre stage. Presaging artisan ice cream makers of the late 1990s and early twenty-first century, Ben & Jerry's, along with Häagen-Dazs and other super-premium brands, strove to create a supremely luxurious product fashioned with natural ingredients. Like Häagen-Dazs, the Vermont ice cream producers upped the butterfat content and squeezed the amount of air. The result was a lavish ice cream that appealed to true aficionados around the world. (Häagen-Dazs and Ben & Jerry's were fierce rivals in the super-premium niche. In 1984, Ben & Jerry's launched the 'What's the Doughboy Afraid of?' campaign against Häagen-Dazs, then owned by Pillsbury, for allegedly trying to limit Ben & Jerry's Boston distribution network.)

And the Vermont ice cream makers added texture to their ice cream. As far back as eighteenth-century French confectioner Emy, ice cream creators had laced their recipes with breadcrumbs or other solid ingredients. But Ben and Jerry's took 'mix-ins', as they were called, to a new level, marbling their ice cream with chunks of candy, cookies and fruits.

The reason for this inventive marrying of textures? It turned out that Cohen had very little sense of taste and smell. By folding in pieces of fruit or candy – and by intensifying the flavours of the ice creams themselves, another Ben & Jerry's hallmark – Cohen, despite his malady, could now easily savour his frozen confections. As it turned out, mixing kooky ingredients into the ice cream base also helped underscore the brand's quirky individuality.

In the 1980s Ben and Jerry decided to establish outlets outside the us. Canada got its first Ben & Jerry's in 1988. In 1994 the product was unveiled in the uk. Two years later, the first of the company's outlets appeared in France. In 1998 the first Ben & Jerry's was launched in Japan.

Today Ben & Jerry's is owned by Unilever, the Anglo-Dutch conglomerate. The two entrepreneurs – Ben and Jerry – maintain offices in Burlington, but they are no longer active in the company's day-to-day operations.

With its worldwide appeal, it's not surprising that movie and TV shows often employ the brand as a handy prop. For example, in the medical TV comedy *Scrubs*, the doctor J.D. comments to a patient that he once got Chunky Monkey in his eye. The characters in the TV series *Friends* frequently gobble up Ben & Jerry's ice-cream. In the movie *Bridget Jones: The Edge of Reason* (2004), the eponymous heroine famously jokes, while eating a Ben & Jerry's ice cream, that she's involved with two men, 'the first named Ben, the other Jerry', while Sandra Bullock, as the lead character in the film *Miss Congeniality* (2000), orders a full pint of Chocolate Chip Cookie Dough.

7

The New Ice Cream Age

Hunky New England Patriots quarterback Tom Brady is super-
model Gisele Bundchen's Mister Softee. The hottest newlyweds
on the planet were shot over the weekend eating ice-cream cones
in Horizontina, Brazil, where they went on their honeymoon.
O Estado de São Paulo, quoted in the *New York Post*, 16 March 2009

In the summer of 2009, a new brand of gelato arrived in New
York. In a bustling metropolis with thousands of outlets dishing up every ice cream variety imaginable – from classic vanilla
to offbeat concoctions like bacon and egg – the debut of yet
another ice cream purveyor caused barely a stir among the
city's ice cream aficionados. But Screme gelato boasted a
unique pedigree. The gelato maker hailed neither from Milan
nor Rome, but rather from a country – Israel – far removed
from the hallowed traditions of Italian gelato making. In
Israel, Screme (known as Aldo's) had assembled more than
50 outlets. Though launched by an Italian gelato maker in
1993, Screme was soon taken over by a group of Israeli businessmen, who quickly rolled out flavours like halva and
lemon to suit local tastes. When Screme opened its New York
outlets, it took its ice cream in yet another direction, fashion-
ing flavours like Captain Crunch, Reese's Peanut Butter and

A rainbow of gelato flavours in a Rome gelateria.

Key Lime Vodka – tastes that were specifically engineered to appeal to American sensibilities.

'The Italians are locked into standard flavors', Screme's owner Yona Levy maintains. Levy hasn't hesitated to aggressively shunt aside centuries-old gelato traditions to create his unique kosher and organic offerings. In fact, it's safe to say that Screme's gelato variant – not to mention its rotating menu of more than 5,000 flavours – would utterly confound Italian ice cream traditionalists.

But Screme's heterodoxy is not unusual. Around the world – from Berlin to Kansas City – globalization has transformed the Italian classic into a frozen dessert that more often than not barely resembles the traditional version. In fact, it could be asked: is today's globalized version of gelato even Italian – or has it been reimagined into an entirely new, universal ice cream type?

Gelato goes global: though gelato shops have sprung up from Kansas City to Berlin, Italy is still home to the world's finest gelato. The Giolitti Ice Cream Parlour in Rome, operating since 1900, typifies the classic gelateria.

Globalization has also wrought changes to classic American ice cream brands and products. Whether it's ice cream on a stick, or a sundae or cone, these ice cream snacks have easily migrated across national borders. There are chocolate-covered bars being peddled in Mumbai and Moscow and ice cream cones in Shanghai. In Japan American brands are very popular. Häagen-Dazs Cookies and Cream and Baskin-Robbins Strawberry Cheesecake stock freezer cases across the country. Yet local variations abound. You can find a mango sundae in Delhi. Green tea and azuki ice cream have stormed Japan. Sometimes, ice cream is partially assimilated, creating old-style treats made in new ways. For instance, in the farming town of Mattituck, Long Island, Pakistani native Ali Choudry has taken over a former Dairy Queen stand. There he whips up Pakistani kulfi, alongside traditional American flavours like Mint Chip and Cookie Dough, for the farmers and winegrowers who frequent his shop. 'It's very popular', says

Choudry, whose kulfi, enriched with rosewater, pistachios and cardamom, is made not from the condensed milk called for by traditional recipes, but from a standard commercial ice cream mix.

Ice cream's universal appeal is underscored by the vast size of today's world ice cream market, which approaches $43 billion, according to research firm Datamonitor. With a quarter of global ice cream sales, some surveys anoint the US the world's leading consumer of ice cream, with Americans downing a total of 3.5 billion litres in 2008 alone. Europeans consumed 3.4 billion litres. Other market research studies have given the nod to New Zealand as the leading ice cream consuming nation. There, according to recent US government statistics, the nation's ice cream lovers devour 28 litres per capita per year, while in the US consumption is

Ice cream vendor, Havana, Cuba, c. 1890–1910. The Coppelia ice cream parlour in Havana has been a favourite gathering spot dating from the decades before the 1959 revolution.

A young woman in Paris enjoying ice cream, 1960.

only slightly less, at 25 litres per capita. In Scandinavia it's 17 litres while in Germany it's a relatively restrained 8 litres per person. Anglo-Dutch Unilever, with 18 per cent of the world ice cream market, and Swiss Nestlé, with 14 per cent, dominate ice cream sales, overseeing iconic brands such as Good Humor and Popsicle (Unilever) and Dreyer's/Edy's and Mövenpick (Nestlé).

Europe

Despite the effects of globalization, Europeans remain loyal to home-grown artisanal products. European sales of ice cream are the largest worldwide, accounting for 43 per cent of the total consumed. Of that amount, artisanal ice creams produced by small concerns make up fully a third of all European revenues, according to Datamonitor. In France, for example, a third of ice cream sales are made by small producers. By contrast, in the us that figure is only 10 per cent.

Still, multinationals have made their mark on European ice cream markets. In the region, the top three large commercial producers are Unilever (20 per cent of the market) and Alliance Agro-Alimentaire and Nestlé, each with 14 per cent.

TOP 10 ICE CREAM MARKETS WORLDWIDE	
MARKET SIZES, IN US$M	2008
USA	15,465.3
Italy	6,489.5
China	5,191
Japan	4,925.8
United Kingdom	3,029.3
Germany	2,813.7
France	2,119.6

South Korea	2,039.8
Canada	1,956.6
Spain	1,854.6

Source: Euromonitor International

Multinationals control about half the total British ice cream market. Yet there's been a recent surge of interest in the artisanal products produced by a growing number of small producers who use natural or organic ingredients in their ice creams. Still, many British ice cream eaters remain staunch traditionalists, according to the Ice Cream Alliance, a British trade group. Those old standbys, vanilla, chocolate and strawberry, continue to rank high among British ice cream fans.

In Italy, the modern ice cream industry originated in Milan in the early 1950s, and today Italians eat more gelato than at any time in the past. Consumption moved steadily upward, increasing from 250 g per person in the 1950s to 7 kg by the late 1990s, according to the Italian Trade Commission.

Mr Whippy's ice cream vans have trolled through the streets of British villages and towns since the mid-twentieth century, bringing treats to children of all ages in refrigerated vans.

A smiling gelato seller in Palermo, Sicily holds up a cone, 2007.

And despite the recent economic downturn, in 2009 Italians spent $1.9 billion on the frozen treat, reported one recent survey. Even the Great Recession of 2009 apparently couldn't put a dent in the world's growing appetite for gelato. In 2009 alone, exports surged 43 per cent, concluded Coldiretti News, an Italian agricultural news service. EU countries, Eastern Europe, China and Japan were the major export markets, the news service said.

Italy is famed for its gelato makers, who produce a high-quality ice cream from the traditional mix of milk, cream, sugar, eggs and flavourings such as chocolate and pistachio and fresh fruits like strawberry. And Italians are devoted to their native ice cream makers. Since 2004 the number of gelaterias has grown nearly 11 per cent to 36,389 gelato-making facilities nationwide, with the strongest growth occurring in central Italy, according to industry statistics.

Small producers dominate the market, crafting about 60 per cent of Italy's gelato – with parents passing the knowledge down to sons and daughters. The Italian Ice Cream Trade Association (AIG) estimates that there are about 37,000 individually owned gelato shops operating in Italy today.

But Italy has not entirely escaped the effects of industrialization. In fact, some gelato makers today incorporate stabilizers, emulsifiers and other artificial ingredients into their products. (During a recent trip to Italy I tasted some divine gelato – and some varieties that were little better than the lowest-quality US supermarket brands.)

Alongside dairy-based gelato, you can also find *sorbetto*, a water-based dessert – perhaps not that different from the water ices the country's pioneering confectioners produced in the sixteenth century – consisting of fruit and sugar that is then frozen. (In Italy, 'gelato' sometimes refers to both milk-based and water-based desserts.)

Gelato differs from regular ice cream in several respects. Gelato's butterfat content ranges between 6 and 8 per cent; for most ice creams, butterfat is between 10 and 16 per cent. Another important distinction between gelato and regular ice cream – and one that accounts in part for gelato's intense creaminess – is the fact that gelato contains almost no air. Also contributing to gelato's consistency is the way it's produced. Forced-air freezers produce an even temperature that helps create a silky texture. Yet another characteristic of gelato is its intense flavour. Silvestro Silvestori, an American cooking instructor living in Lecco, Italy and a gelato maker himself, explains that this is 'because gelato is not frozen as hard' as regular ice cream; flavours are therefore deep and rich.

Stored in long, flat containers, gelato is scooped with a paddle. Traditional gelato flavours – many gelaterias offer only a small selection of flavours – include pistachio, chocolate, coffee, lemon, strawberry and stracciatella.

Unlike in the US and parts of Western Europe, Italians tend to eschew ice cream for dessert. 'Finishing a meal with ice cream would be pretty rare', says Silvestori. Instead, most Italians enjoy their gelato as an afternoon or evening snack. And in parts of Sicily, gelato is sometimes even eaten for breakfast. There, diners munch on a kind of Sicilian ice cream sandwich – a brioche filled with gelato.

These days, gelato is travelling the globe. There are stands and cafés from Chicago to Berlin. In the US gelato is starting to gain a toehold. In New York a gelato stand can even be found in one of the city's commuter railroad stations. Kansas City, in the US heartland, can point to at least three gelato shops, some offering daring takes on the traditional Italian confection. (Paciugo Gelato's Amarena Cordial milkshake fuses chocolate chip gelato with Black Cherry Swirl ice cream.) These days, growing numbers of Americans are warming to the idea of gelato. One recent survey, by research firm Mintel, found that close to a majority, 45 per cent of those polled, favoured the consistency of gelato over that of ice cream – and more than a third said it tasted better than the typical US ice cream. Italian gelato companies have also entered the American market. Base and flavour maker Pergel, for example, has set up US operations. It ships its products around the US and holds training courses for aspiring American gelato makers.

Russia

Despite its frigid climate, Russia can claim a long history of ice cream eating. Catherine the Great was an ice cream devotee. In fact, the Czarina was known to possess an elaborate ice cream service, consisting of a painted and gilded ice cream cooler with two nesting bowls made of Sèvres porcelain, as well as various utensils.

The modern-day Russian ice cream industry dates back to the 1930s; by the middle of the decade, Soviet factories were turning out 12 tons of the icy dessert a year. When economic woes plagued Russia in the 1990s, ice cream consumption plummeted. Today, however, with better economic times, eating ice cream – chocolate covered bars on sticks, cones and sandwiches are all popular items – is on the upswing, and each Russian downs about three kilograms of ice cream per year. However, Russians still lag behind other countries with more established ice cream-consuming traditions. Russians eat about half as much ice cream as Western Europeans, and about a quarter the amount consumed in the US. Traditionally, small Russian producers, like Russky, Kholod and Talosto, and Inmarko, have dominated the country's ice cream market. Lately, however, multinationals have gained a foothold. In February 2008, for example, Unilever announced that it would acquire Inmarko.

Turkey

In Turkey, a venerable ice cream tradition dates back at least three hundred years. 'Dondurma', which literally translates to 'freezing', is the Turkish word for ice cream. Turkish confectioners concoct a mixture that incorporates flour milled from the wild orchids (*salepi* or *salep*) found in the southeastern parts of Turkey. *Salepi* is derived from the Arabic *sahlab*, and orchid ice cream can also be found in other parts of the Middle East. The literal translation of *salepi* is 'fox testicles', so in Turkey if you eat ice cream, you're dining on an unusual dish indeed!

An ice cream merchant in Constantinople, Turkey, *c.* 1898.

Turkish ice cream is thicker and more elastic than Western versions and is sometimes so tough that one requires a knife and fork to eat it. To create *salepi dondurma*, street vendors use metal paddles to whip milk, sugar and mastic resin along with the *salepi* into a smooth but chewy consistency. Sometimes vendors dip cones in crushed pistachios.

Today Turkish ice cream manufacturers, including companies from the Maras region, an area renowned for the high quality of its ice cream, manufacture commercial varieties of *salepi dondurma*. But the Turks' appetite for ice cream appears to have expanded beyond their native dish. Total sales of Turkish and standard varieties of ice cream are expected to reach $821 million in 2008, up 13 per cent in just one year, according to Euromonitor. US government studies have found that local per capita ice cream consumption, currently 2.7 litres per person, has doubled over the last five years. Some of that growth has been fuelled by wealthy city-dwellers' yearning for international super-premium brands, like Häagen-Dazs and Ben & Jerry's, which market worldwide favourites like Chunky Monkey and Cookie Dough to upscale Turkish ice cream lovers. Other multinationals are entering the Turkish market as well; in 2008, Unilever's Sanayii ve Ticaret Türk AS led all other ice cream makers in sales revenues. Still, despite the proliferation of brands, in Turkey, most people consume ice cream in the summer months. According to a January 2009 Euromonitor report, there's a widespread belief among Turks that eating ice cream during the frigid winter months can spark maladies such as throat infections.

Middle East

Though a stark political divide separates Arabs and Israelis, ice cream is a passion shared by both sides. In the Arab Middle East, in countries such as Iran and Syria, orchid ice cream similar to the Turkish variety is enjoyed. There is also *bouzat haleeb*, typically fashioned from mastic and flavoured with rose water; this ice cream boasts a stretchy consistency.

Fuelled by higher incomes, growing numbers of Arab consumers today consider ice cream an affordable luxury. Today, in Arab countries such as Saudi Arabia and Dubai, Western ice cream brands, including Ben & Jerry's, Baskin-Robbins and Mövenpick, are all the rage. In January 2009 Baskin-Robbins opened its hundredth outlet in the United Arab Emirates. Even in war-torn Iraq, ice cream demonstrates a potent allure.

Just three years after the state of Israel was formed in 1948, Strauss-Elite Ltd, now a Unilever subsidiary and the largest Israeli ice cream producer, began operations. Today premium flavours like green tea and white chocolate abound. In Israel ice cream is so popular that demand for the treat shot ahead nine per cent in 2008 alone. Cones and other novelties are strong sellers, but local influences abound, with flavours such as halva and poppy seed served up at numerous scoop shops. Ice cream constructions tied to the country's historical landmarks are not unknown. According to a *Haaretz* newspaper report in 2007, one vendor created a dessert called Damascus Gate (after Jerusalem's Old City entrance), a melange layered with halva ice cream, shredded halva, raw tehina and pine nuts.

The Asia-Pacific Region

For a look at ice cream's future, search no further than the Asia-Pacific region – Japan, India, China, Australia and New Zealand. By 2013, total sales are expected to reach $14.1 billion in the vast area – a staggering increase of 29 per cent in just five years, Datamonitor reports.

The Japanese have been fervent ice cream partisans for years, while Australia and New Zealand always rank near the top of most lists of the world's greatest ice cream-consuming countries. And despite widespread lactose intolerance among the Chinese, the country nevertheless accounts for 40 per cent of all sales in the region's ice cream market. Meanwhile, newly affluent Indians, where kulfi is the traditional frozen dessert, are also developing an appetite for Western brands and styles of ice cream.

Ice cream was said to have been introduced to Japan in 1869 after the Japanese shogun was introduced to the frozen dessert during a visit to the US. The ruler was said 'to have marveled at its taste', according to a history of Japanese ice cream compiled by the Japanese Ice Cream Association. One account of the occasion, which took place on a ship docked in Philadelphia, the shogun described how the ice cream he tasted 'melts in the mouth immediately'.

Teenager eating an ice cream cone, Hanoi, Vietnam, 2009.

The first ice cream manufactured in Japan was produced in Yokohama. Ice and salt from the city's roadways were deployed to make this early Japanese ice cream. In 1900, the Shiseido ice cream parlour opened in Tokyo, 'imitating the American drugstore', as the Japanese Ice Cream Association puts it. The Tokyo establishment served sodas and sundaes, and by 1921 the Japanese had begun commercial production of ice cream. Still, in these early years, ice cream was a luxury for many ordinary Japanese. By the 1930s ice cream vendors peddling through Japanese cities on tricycles became common-place; large-scale commercial manufacturing of ice cream also took hold. During this period, 'Three colour ice' – chocolate, strawberry and lemon – was a widely sold brand marketed by Snow Brand and other commercial producers.

During the Second World War, ice cream manufacturing came to a virtual halt in Japan, but it resumed in the mid-1950s. Ice lollies or popsicles were sold and in 1953, Snow Brand Shinagawa started producing small cups filled with ice

Matcha tea ice cream is just one of the unusual flavours that the ice cream-loving Japanese have invented.

cream. Today the Japanese market accounts for roughly a quarter of all ice cream sold in the Asia-Pacific region. In Japan standard Western flavours like vanilla are favourites. Other top selling flavours include *matcha* (green tea), azuki beans, *kurogoma* (black sesame seeds), *kinako* (powdered, roasted soy beans), *tonyu* (soy milk) and *kuromitsu* (brown sugar syrup), according to Yukari Sakamoto, a Japanese journalist and author. Crab, sea urchin, wasabi (horseradish), beef tongue, curry, octopus, eel, kelp and garlic are other sought-after flavours.

Meanwhile, over the years, there's been an influx of multinationals into the island nation. Häagen-Dazs' first shop opened in 1984, while Baskin-Robbins, which has been operating in Japan for more than 30 years, now boasts over 850 locations, the company's largest number of outlets outside the

An Indian abdar, or water carrier, preparing cold drinks, *c.* 1790s. Iced drinks were the precursor of ices and sorbets.

US. A recent arrival is Cold Stone Creamery, whose 'mix-ins' – candy, cakes and other solids – have won over Japanese consumers.

To woo Japanese ice cream devotees, global brands offer a mélange of Eastern- and Western-themed treats. In a nod to Japanese tastes, Häagen-Dazs, for example, features green tea and melon flavoured ice creams, but Western favourites, such as Cookies and Cream and Almond Praline Cream, are also popular. At Baskin-Robbins stores, classics like New York Cheesecake and Rocky Road occupy space in freezer cases alongside Japanese-inspired offerings like *matcha*, musk melon and azuki.

Unlike Japan, India boasts a venerable indigenous ice cream culture. Mughal emperors enjoyed flavoured ice brought down from nearby mountains. Later, confectioners developed kulfi, a milk-based dish. Kulfi isn't churned like Western-style ice cream. Instead, the mixture is cooked, then frozen in small metal cones. The result is a dense, chewy dish.

Throughout India, street vendors or *kulfiwala*s sell kulfi – recipes vary but kulfi is often made from sweetened condensed milk, cream and sugar and flavourings such as pistachios, cardamom and saffron – from carts where they keep it cold in pots called *matka*.

In recent years, kulfi, while widely consumed, has had to compete in the Indian marketplace with Western-style ice creams. Newly affluent Indians benefiting from the country's recent spurt of economic growth, are now clamouring for cups, cones and other packaged ice cream delights. Häagen-Dazs opened its first outlet in 2009, and plans as many as 40 cafés and shops in the coming years. (Gelato Vittorio, Delhi's first *gelateria*, opened its doors in 2007.) In fact, Indian sales of ice cream skyrocketed by 23 per cent between 2006 and 2007, according to Euromonitor, which concluded that India could 'remain the fastest growing country in the Asia-Pacific

A *kulfiwala*, or ice cream vendor, mans his cart in Fort Cochin, India, 2007.

region for ice cream sales'. So popular is ice cream among India's growing middle class that a museum dedicated to the frozen treat opened its doors in 2007. Located in the Nirula ice cream factory (in the 1970s, the company pioneered ice cream parlours in India), the museum sports ice cream facts, games and trivia.

Yet despite its newfound celebrity, ice cream's success in India faces some daunting challenges. Enormous numbers of Indians remain mired in poverty. And the country's huge landmass makes it difficult to expand ice cream franchises. But while the cities are benefiting most from the influx of ice cream brands, companies like Gujarat Co-operative Milk Marketing Federation Ltd (GCMMF), which markets the Amul ice cream brand, are also moving aggressively into rural areas. Their flavours and novelties evince a decidedly Indian influence. For example, Rajbhog, a combination of nuts, honey and saffron, is a traditional play on Indian flavours, while mango, lychee and pineapple also boast a homegrown appeal. Meanwhile, the company also sells Western-style ice cream bars, nut-and-chocolate-covered cones and sundaes.

In China, the country's burgeoning middle class, with its appetite for Western-style indulgences, is fuelling the growth of the native ice cream industry. In 1980, following the end of the Cultural Revolution, the Dong Fang Department Store in Beijing offered ice cream sodas for the first time in fourteen years. So great was the pent-up demand for the treat that the shop sold 1,500 sodas in the first three days alone, the *New York Times* reported in June 1980.

These days, the Chinese down a fifth of the world's total production of ice cream, according to a 2005 report by the US Department of Agriculture. Indeed, ice cream's Western roots lend it a considerable cachet in the eyes of many Chinese consumers. The Chinese feast on chocolate-covered

Ice cream and obesity: manufacturers around the world are developing lines of sugar-free and low-fat products. This Malaysian poster warns against the dangers of too much sugar.

bars, not to mention ever greater amounts of premium brand products like Häagen-Dazs, which boasts more than twenty outlets in the country, serving flavours ranging from green tea to dulce de leche. Wedding cakes, ice cream cakes and other delicacies abound. (Lately, the Chinese have developed such an appetite for super-premium ice cream that consumption shot up 35 per cent in just one year.)

Given the enormous market potential, Nestlé and Unilever are racing to capture the exploding Chinese ice cream market, which in 2007 grew 11 per cent, reaching sales of HK$1 billion a year later, reports Euromonitor. With billions of potential ice cream customers at stake, even relatively small players, such as Philadelphia's Bassetts, have entered the thriving Chinese ice cream market. And domestic players, like Yili, continue to sell products despite the recent melamine food safety scare, in which thousands fell ill or died after drinking milk contaminated with the compound.

Though many Chinese have become ardent ice cream partisans, barriers to acceptance remain. For one, dairy is not a part of traditional Chinese cuisine. For another, lactose intolerance is nearly universal. And the hot climate, not to mention the existence of daunting transportation and refrigeration challenges, also have hobbled growth. Only a small percentage of homeowners own freezers. And sanitary conditions remain problematic.

In Australia, ice cream is beloved and the country almost always ranks near the top of the world's top consuming nations. Australian ice cream lovers have an American to thank for introducing ice cream to their country. Pining for the ice cream he had encountered in his native state of Michigan, Frederick Peters used his mother's recipe to make the frosty treat in his backyard shed in Sydney. Soon, in 1907, he established Peters' American Delicacy Company. Now a subsidiary of Nestlé, Peters remains one of Australia's major ice cream brands. Even today, some of Peters' iconic novelties – including the Drumstick, Choc Wedge and Dixie Cup – are cherished among Down Under ice cream aficionados.

Prized for the high quality of their dairy products, New Zealanders devour around 22 litres of ice cream per person, reports the New Zealand Ice Cream Manufacturers' Association. A favourite flavour is hokey pokey, which consists of vanilla ice cream studded with chunks of toffee. Only vanilla outranks it in popularity.

Ice Cream Tomorrow: A Culinary Replay

These days, supermarket freezers around the world are bulging with an ever-expanding array of commercially produced ice cream brands. But hand-crafted varieties, harking back to the time before industrialization when ice cream was a simple amalgam of sugar, cream and flavourings, are staging a comeback. These craft producers fashion small batches of ice cream, generally for local consumption. Eschewing stabilizers, emulsifiers and other artificial additives, artisan makers mix together fresh, locally produced cream, eggs and flavourings. Ingredients are often organic and coffee, chocolate and other flavours may be sourced from Fair Trade growers. Deluxe ingredients abound – from gourmet chocolate and real vanilla beans to local maple syrup. A new burst of extravagant flavours has enlivened the contemporary ice cream scene, as well. From olive to sweetcorn, ice cream makers are enlivening the treats with unusual accents. Even the lowly ice pop is displaying a newfound lustre. Brooklyn concern People's Pops crafts all-natural fruit ices on a stick from locally grown ingredients, including watermelon, cucumber and hyssop. And

Ice cream cone on the rocks.

today's ice cream-making wizardry would astound the most daring soda jerk of yore. These days, some ice cream chefs are borrowing a page from micro-gastronomy. They're turning to liquid nitrogen to produce 'instant' ice cream flavours right in their shops.

These sophisticated brands – targeted at gourmand elites – star in a replay of early ice cream history when the frozen confection was a delicacy that only the affluent could afford. A niche offering, today's artisan-made ice creams are almost always pricier than supermarket brands. But despite their higher cost, the number of artisan brands is growing. In the UK and Ireland alone, according to the Ice Cream Alliance, there are about 1,000 small makers – including ones like Top House Dairy Ice Cream in Shropshire and Helsett Farm in Cornwall.

Even the humble ice cream truck and the venerable soda fountain are staging a revival of sorts. Fans clamour for vintage

Tomato and basil ice cream in an ice cream parlour in Nice, France, 2007. Today's ice cream makers are infusing ice cream with ever more daring flavour accents.

ice cream experiences. Today, you can still find a few relics of ice cream's golden age sprinkled here and there on America's Main Streets. In Philadelphia the Franklin Fountain is a recreation of the authentic ice cream soda fountain. Opened only in 2004, the modern-day parlour, like the fountains of yore, places a premium on ice cream showmanship with inventive takes on traditional fountain treats, such as the Mt Vesuvius sundae, a mound of chocolate or vanilla ice cream 'erupting' with chocolate brownie pieces, hot fudge and malt powder. And vintage soda fountains are making a comeback as well. In the Long Island town of Riverhead, New York, for example, the Meras family continues to operate the 90-year-old Star Confectionery. Adorned with its original stained-glass windows and white marble counter, the old-time eatery draws nostalgia-seekers from all over the New York area. 'We still have generations of families who come here for an ice cream cone and a sundae', said Anthony Meras, the third generation of his family to operate the beloved ice cream parlour.

Meanwhile, ice cream trucks are staging a comeback as well. In New York, for example, Van Leeuwen Artisan Ice Cream fields a small fleet of sunny yellow trucks from which it dispenses its silky, luxurious ice cream. And there's the Big, Gay Ice Cream truck; it prowls the city serving up ice cream creations boasting unusual toppings like Toasted Curried Coconut.

Not surprisingly, mainstream brands are responding to consumers' newfound craving for high-quality, luxurious ice creams. Häagen-Dazs' new Five product (the ice creams are made with just five ingredients) cater to sophisticated ice cream enthusiasts. In the Five line, unusual flavours like caramel, ginger and passion fruit convey the idea that this ice cream isn't just for kids. Ginger, for example, is described on the Häagen-Dazs website as 'refreshing, with a slightly warm kick of flavor', while coffee contains 'the taste of Brazilian coffee beans brewed to perfection'.

Then there are producers who aim to serve the millions of ice cream lovers worldwide who have trouble digesting cow's milk dairy products. Roughly 70 per cent of the world's population suffers from some degree of lactose intolerance – the inability to digest the sugar in dairy products. Europeans boast a low rate of lactose intolerance. For instance, in Belgium, Ireland, Netherlands, Sweden and the UK, only about five per cent of the population suffers from the affliction, according to industry statistics. Meanwhile, Asians – including citizens of China and Japan, among the world's most passionate ice cream eaters – experience lactase deficiency rates that are close to 100 per cent.

To satisfy the demand for non-dairy 'ice creams', companies like Soy Delicious and Tofutti in the US market soy-based frozen desserts, while other producers, like US producer Laloo, market goat's milk ice cream in exotic flavours, including Black Mission Fig and Rumplemint.

At the other end of the spectrum reside low-calorie and low-fat ice creams. Ice cream fans crave the richness of the frozen treat – but they aim to avoid its fat and calories. And with more than a billion obese adults worldwide, according to the World Health Organization, ice cream manufacturers are responding with an expanding menu of 'healthier' ice cream products.

Even so, with sugar or without, high fat or low, super-premium or supermarket brand, ice cream will always stand alone as the world's favourite treat. It's a sinful indulgence that few would choose to go without.

Recipes

Mary Eales's Ice Cream
—from *Mrs Mary Eales's Receipts* (London, 1733), p. 92

Take Tin Ice-Pots, fill them with any Sort of Cream you like, either plain or sweeten'd, or Fruit in it; shut your Pots very close; to six Pots you must allow eighteen or twenty Pound of Ice, breaking the Ice very small; there will be some great Pieces, which lay at the Bottom and Top: You must have a Pail, and lay some Straw at the Bottom; then lay in your Ice, and put in amongst it a Pound of Bay-Salt; set in your Pots of Cream, and lay Ice and Salt between every Pot, that they may not touch; but the Ice must lie round them on every Side; lay a good deal of Ice on the Top, cover the Pail with Straw, set it in a Cellar where no Sun or Light comes, it will be froze in four Hours, but it may stand longer; than take it out just as you use it; hold it in your Hand and it will slip out. When you wou'd freeze any Sort of Fruit, either Cherries, Rasberries, Currants, or Strawberries, fill your Tin-Pots with the Fruit, but as hollow as you can; put to them Lemmon-ade, made with Spring-Water and Lemmon-Juice sweeten'd; put enough in the Pots to make the Fruit hang together, and put them in Ice as you do Cream.

Hannah Glasse's Ice-cream

—from *The Art Of Cookery, Made Plain And Easy* (London, 1755),

p. 332.

Take two pewter-basons, one larger than the other the inward one must have a close cover, into which you are to put your cream, and mix it with raspberries, or whatever you like best, to give it a flavour and a colour. Sweeten it to your palate; then cover it close, and set it into the larger bason. Fill it with ice, and a handful of salt: let it stand in this ice three quarters of an hour, then uncover it, and stir the cream well together; cover it close again, and let it stand half an hour longer, after that turn it into your plate. These things are made at the pewterers.

Richard Briggs's Ice Cream

—from Richard Briggs, *The New Art Of Cookery* (Philadelphia, PA,

1792), pp. 399–400

Take a dozen ripe apricots, pare them very thin and stone them, scald and put them into a mortar, and beat them fine; put to them six ounces of double-refined sugar, a pint of scaling cream, and rub it through a sieve with the back of a spoon; then put it into a tin with a close cover, and set it in a tub of ice broken small, with four handsful of salt mixt among the ice; when you see your cream get thick round the edges of your tin, stir it well, and put it in again till it becomes quite thick; when the cream is all froze up, take it out of the tin, and put it into the mould you intend to turn it out of; mind that you put a piece of paper on each end, between the lids and the ice cream, put on the top lid, and have another tub of ice ready, as before, put the mould in the middle, with the ice under and over it; let it stand four hours, and do not turn it out before you want it; then dip the mould into cold spring water, take off the lids and paper, and turn it into a plate. You may do any sort of fruit the same way.

Monticello Ice Cream

—from Jefferson Papers, Library of Congress and
www.monticello.org/jefferson/dayinlife/dining/at.html

2 bottles of good cream
6 yolks of eggs
½ lb. sugar

Mix the yolks & sugar put the cream on a fire in a casserole, first putting in a stick of Vanilla. When near boiling take it off & pour it gently into the mixture of eggs & sugar. Stir it well. Put it on the fire again stirring it thoroughly with a spoon to prevent it's sticking to the casserole. When near boiling take it off and strain it thro' a towel. Put it in the Sabottiere [the inner can used in an ice pail], then set it in ice an hour before it is to be served. Put into the ice a handful of salt. Put salt on the coverlid of the Sabotiere & cover the whole with ice. Leave it still half a quarter of an hour. Then turn the Sabottiere in the ice 10 minutes. Open it to loosen with a spatula the ice from the inner sides of the Sabotiere. Shut it & replace it in the ice. Open it from time to time to detach the ice from the sides. When well taken, stir it well with the Spatula. Put it in moulds, jostling it well down on the knee. Then put the mould into the same bucket of ice. Leave it there to the moment of serving it. To withdraw it, immerse the mould in warm water, turning it well till it will come out & turn it into a plate.

A Lady of Philadelphia's Ice Cream

—from *Seventy-five Receipts for Pastry, Cakes, and Sweetmeats* (Boston, MA, 1828), p. 37

A quart of rich cream.
Half a pound of powdered loaf-sugar.
The juice of two large lemons, or a pint of
strawberries or raspberries.

Put the cream into a broad pan, and squeeze the lemon juice into it, or stir in gradually the strawberries or raspberries, which must first be mashed to a smooth paste. Then stir in the sugar by degrees, and when all is well mixed, strain it through a sieve.

Put it into a tin that has a close cover, and set it in a tub. Fill the tub with ice broken into very small pieces, and strew among the ice a large quantity of salt, taking care that none of the salt gets into the cream. Scrape the cream down with a spoon as it freezes round the edges of the tin. When it is all frozen, dip the tin in lukewarm water; take out the ice cream, and fill your glasses; but not till a few minutes before you want to use it, as it will very soon melt.

You may heighten the colour of the red fruit, by a little cochineal.

If you wish to have it in moulds, put the cream into them as soon as it has frozen in the tin. Set the moulds in a tub of ice and salt. Just before you want to use the cream, take the moulds out of the tub, wipe or wash the slat, carefully from the outside, dip the moulds in lukewarm water, and turn out the cream.

Cinnamon, Ginger or Pumpernickel Ice Cream
(*Glace Crème à la Canelle, au Gingembre ou au Pumpernickel Pain de Seigle*)
—from Charles Ranhofer, *The Epicurean* (New York, 1894), p. 987

With Cinnamon. infuse one ounce of cinnamon in a quart of boiling milk. Place twelve ounces of sugar in a basin with eight egg yolks; beat and add the infusion; mix so that the sugar dissolves, cook without boiling, then cool and pass through a fine sieve; freeze and mix in a few vanilla chocolate pastilles, each half an inch in diameter.

Ginger. Substitute ginger for the cinnamon and finish the same.

Pumpernickel Rye Bread. Grate half a pound of rye bread and pass it through a coarse sieve or colander; pour into a vessel and throw over a pint of thirty-degree syrup. Break twelve egg-yolks in a tin basin, add eight ounces of sugar, mix well with a pint of boiling milk; cook this on a slow fire without boiling, remove and when cold strain through a sieve, freeze, adding the rye bread when nearly frozen and two quarts of whipped cream.

Ice Cream Cones

—from Mrs C. Vinton Henry, 'Dishes That Will Make Men Love Homes', *Chicago Daily Tribune*, 3 November 1907, p. f3

One-fourth of a cupful of butter, one-half of a cupful of powdered sugar, one-fourth of a cupful of milk, seven-eighths of a cupful of flour, one-half teaspoonful of vanilla.

Cream the butter, add the sugar, and cream them well together; then add the milk slowly and last add the flour and flavoring. Spread this with a broad bladed knife on the bottom of a square or oblong tin. Bake until light brown, then cut in large squares and roll up, beginning at one corner, like a cornucopia. If the squares become to [sic] brittle to roll up, place them in the oven again to soften. The lower end must be pinched together.

Mrs. T. W. Schroeder won a $1 prize for this recipe.

Vanilla Ice Cream (Philadelphia)

—from Fannie Merritt Farmer, *The Boston Cooking-School Cookbook* (Boston, MA, 1896), p. 372

1 quart thin cream.
¾ cup sugar.
1 ½ tablespoons vanilla.

Mix ingredients, and freeze.

Chocolate Ice Cream Soda

—from Theodore Kay, former soda jerk and drugstore owner,
via Anne Coglianese

Take a tall soda glass and give it 1 and ½ shots of syrup (chocolate). A fast spray of seltzer – push back on the handle – and 2 scoops of ice cream, usually vanilla. Slow spray (forward pull) of seltzer to the top and a dash of whip cream. Long spoon and a straw.

Purple Cow

—from Marian Manners, 'Folder Tells of Ice Cream Novelties',
Los Angeles Times, 21 April 1946, p. c6.

½ c chilled grape juice
2 T sugar
1 T milk
Chilled ginger ale
2 large servings of vanilla ice cream.

Put the grape juice in a tall glass, add sugar, milk and stir well. Add one-half cup ginger ale and one serving ice cream; stir well. Add three-fourths glass more ginger ale. Add another serving of ice cream. Serves one.

Over the Top Sundae

—from Arthur L. Buzzell, ed., *The Bulletin of Pharmacy*
(Detroit, MI, 1918), p. 210

On a small platter put two No. 16 cones of vanilla ice cream and put a piece of nougat candy between the cones. Over one pour some maple dressing, over the other sprinkle some nut meats and top with whipped cream.

Chop Suey Sauce for Sundaes

—from Albert Allis Hopkins, *The Scientific American Cyclopedia of Formulas* (New York, 1910), p. 312

Half pound of figs chopped into small pieces, 1 pound of seeded dates cut up, 1 pound of English walnuts broken, but not too fine. Add syrup enough to make 2 quarts, color dark red. Fill a sundae glass two-thirds full of ice cream, pour over it a large ladle of chop suey, a little whipped cream and a cherry on top.

Banana Split

—from Will O. Rigby, Fred Rigby, *Rigby's Reliable Candy Teacher: With Complete and Modern Soda, Ice Cream and Sherbet Sections . . . ,* 13th edn (Topeka, KS, 1920), p. 239

Peel a solid banana and split it into two parts. Lay one of these parts on each side of an oblong glass or china tray then between the two, place a disher of vanilla ice cream, a disher of chocolate ice cream and a disher of strawberry ice cream. Over the strawberry, pour crushed strawberries; over the chocolate, crushed pineapple; and over the plain ice cream, crushed cherries. Sprinkle lightly with nuts. Top with whipped cream.

Ice Cream Flower Pots

—from 'Ice Cream Lends Self to Clever Party Desserts', *Chicago Daily Tribune* (10 July 1936), p. 18

Cut brick ice cream into cubes about 3 inches high. Press thin chocolate filled wafers around the sides of the ice cream, sprinkle the top with chocolate shot for soil, and stick a tiny spray of artificial flowers into the center top. Instead of the posies you can achieve very tricky little gumdrop plants by sticking a tiny gumdrop on the end of each branch of a little twisty twig plucked from one of your pet garden shrubs.

Bohemian Girl

—from Will O. Rigby, Fred Rigby, *Rigby's Reliable Candy Teacher*, 13th edn (Topeka, KS, 1920), p. 240

In the middle of a six-inch tray, lay a slice of crystallized or sliced pineapple, then on top of this, place a disher of vanilla ice cream. Now over the ice cream, pour a ladle of sliced peaches, then liberally pour whipped cream over the peaches. Run lady fingers that have been halved up the sides of the ice cream so that they all run toward the peak of the ice cream. Top with a large red cherry, place pecan and English walnuts between the lady fingers, but do not overdo this. Garnish sides of tray with fresh mint leaves and you have one of the most palatable and tempting dishes possible.

Chocolate Marshmallow Sundae

—from 'Here are Recipes for Ice Cream and Sauce that Take the Care', *Chicago Daily Tribune*, 14 May 1937, p. 23

Chocolate Ice Cream
16 marshmallows
1 square unsweetened chocolate
1 c milk
3 T sugar
1 tsp vanilla
Pinch of salt
1 c whipping cream

Place marshmallows, chipped chocolate and milk into a double boiler and steam until the marshmallows and chocolates are melted. Add sugar, vanilla and salt. Cool. When cold and slightly stiffened, fold in the stiffly whipped cream and turn into freezing trays of mechanical refrigerator and freeze without stirring.

Marshmallow Sauce
20 marshmallows
1 c sugar
1–2 c water
3 T cream
1 tsp vanilla

Melt marshmallows with cream in top of double boiler. Boil sugar and water together until syrup spins a thread. Add to marshmallow mixture. Blend until smooth. Add vanilla and serve on ice cream.

Chocolate Sauce
—from 'Timely Tested Recipes from The Bureau of Home Economics, Department of Agriculture', *Washington Post*, 29 March 1931, p. MF12

2 squares unsweetened chocolate
1 c granulated sugar
½ c milk
1 T butter
⅛ tsp salt
½ tsp vanilla

Melt the chocolate in a double boiler, add the sugar, milk, butter and salt, and cook for 10 minutes or until fairly thick. Add the vanilla, beat well, and serve hot over ice cream.

Modern Recipes

Sweet Corn Ice Cream

—with permission of Claudia Fleming, co-owner and pastry chef,
The North Fork Table & Inn; former pastry chef,
Gramercy Tavern, New York; James Beard Award winner,
Pastry Chef of the Year, 2000.

4 ears of sweet summer corn (preferably white)
2 cups (500 ml) whole milk
2 cups (500 ml) heavy cream
¾ cup (150 g) granulated sugar
8 large egg yolks

Slice the kernels off the corncobs and place in a large saucepot. Break the cobs into thirds and add them to the pot along with the milk, cream and half the sugar. Bring the mixture to a boil. Remove from the heat and remove the corncobs.

Using an immersion blender, puree the corn. Return the cobs to the pot to infuse for approximately one hour.

Bring the mixture back to the heat and allow it to come to a scald. Turn off the heat. In a small bowl whisk the yolks with the remaining sugar. Slowly add 1 cup of the corn mixture to the yolks whisking constantly. Add the yolk mixture to the saucepot whisking. Cook over medium low heat, stirring continuously with a heatproof rubber spatula until the mixture thickens enough to coat the back of a spoon.

Pass the custard through a fine sieve, pressing down on the solids; discard solids. Cool custard in an ice bath, then cover and chill at least 4 hours. Freeze in an ice cream maker according to the manufacturer's instructions.

Roquefort and Honey Ice Cream

—with the permission of Chef David Lebovitz, author of *Room For Dessert, Ripe For Dessert, The Great Book of Chocolate* and *The Perfect Scoop*

6 tablespoons honey
4 ounces (110 g) Roquefort
1 cup (250 ml) heavy cream
1 cup (250 ml) whole milk
4 large egg yolks
a few turns freshly ground black pepper

In a small saucepan warm the honey, then set aside. Crumble the Roquefort into a large bowl. Set a mesh strainer over the top. In a medium saucepan, warm the milk.

In a separate bowl, whisk together the egg yolks. Slowly pour the warm milk into the egg yolks, whisking constantly. Scrape the warmed egg yolks back into the saucepan. Over medium heat, stir the mixture constantly with a wooden spoon or heatproof spatula, scraping the bottom as you stir, until the mixture thickens and coats the spoon. Pour the custard through the strainer and stir it into the cheese. Stir until most of the cheese is melted (some small bits are fine, and rather nice in the finished ice cream.) Stir in the cream and the honey, and add a few turns of black pepper. Chill custard thoroughly, then freeze in your ice cream maker according to the manufacturer's instructions.

Coconut Ice Cream Sandwich

—with the permission of Chef Pichet Ong, The Village Tart, and Spot dessert bar, New York

Coconut Sheet Cookie for Sandwich
3 eggs, room temperature
1 cup (200 g) sugar
1/8 tsp salt
2 1/2 cups (230 g) coconut flakes

To make the coconut cookie: preheat the oven to 300°F (150°C). Spray two quarter sheet pans (6.5in. × 4.5in. × 0.5in.) with non-stick cooking spray, line with parchment paper, and spray again. Put the eggs, lime zest, sugar, and salt into the bowl of an electric mixer fitted with the whisk attachment. Whisk on medium speed until thick, pale yellow, and doubled in volume, 8 minutes. Stir in the vanilla extract and gently fold in the coconut.

Spread the batter evenly into the prepared baking sheets and bake until fragrant and golden brown, 15–18 minutes. Remove from the oven and cool in the pan completely until the cookie is hard when touched, then invert into a large cutting board.

Transfer one of the sheet cookies onto the quarter sheet pan, inverting it upside down so the browned crust side is at the bottom. Reserve the other sheet until ice cream is ready to be assembled.

Coconut Ice-cream
¾ cup (170 g, 6 fl. oz) whole milk
¾ cup (170 g, 6 fl. oz) coconut milk
1½ cups (130 g, 4¼ oz) finely shredded unsweetened dried coconut
¾ cup (150 g, 5¼ oz) sugar
8 large egg yolks
¼ tsp salt
1¼ cups (336 g, 12 fl. oz.) heavy whipping cream (double cream)
3 tablespoons coconut-flavoured rum (optional)

Put the milk, coconut milk, dried coconut, sugar and salt in a medium saucepan and set over medium heat. Bring to a steady simmer and cook, stirring occasionally, for 8 minutes. Let mixture sit until it comes to room temperature, about an hour. Break yolks with a whisk and set aside until later.

Bring mixture to boil again and pour ½ cup of the warm milk mixture onto the yolks in a slow, steady stream, whisking constantly. Transfer the yolk mixture back to the saucepan, set over low heat, and cook, stirring constantly, until the mixture is thick enough to coat the back of a spoon and registers 165°F (75°C), about 5 minutes. Remove from the heat and strain the mixture through a fine-mesh sieve into a large mixing bowl, then pour the cream through the sieve, squeezing the coconut flakes to extract as much liquid as possible. Stir in the rum. Set the mixture over a larger bowl of ice and water and cool, stirring occasionally, until cool to the touch, about 40°F (4°C). Alternatively, cover and refrigerate until cold.

Transfer the mixture to your ice cream maker and follow the manufacturer's instructions.

Assembly

Use an offset metal spatula to spread churned ice cream over the sheet cookie until covered. Place the other sheet cookie on top and gently press down to stick to the ice cream. Cover the entire ice cream sandwich tightly with plastic wrap. Once frozen, remove from freezer and invert onto a large cutting board. Cut ice cream sandwich into square pieces of about 2" x 2". Cut each square diagonally into two triangles and serve immediately.

Serves 6–8.

Aonori Ice Cream

—with the permission of Chef Yumiko Kano, the owner of the vegetarian kaiseki restaurant Sen in Tokyo and author of 17 cookbooks focusing on the rich vegetarian cuisine of Japan, and with the assistance of journalist Yukari Sakamoto, author of *Food Sake Tokyo* (The Little Bookroom, New York, 2010).

Ingredients:
8 grams (¼ oz) dried aonori
¼ cup (60 ml) soy milk
4 tablespoons sweet white wine
300 grams (11 oz) amazake
1 teaspoon lemon juice
dash of salt

* Note that the amazake should be without added sugar, and the thick style. This may be hard to find outside of Japan.

Combine all ingredients in a food processor and mix until incorporated. Place the mixture into shallow metal pan and put into the freezer. After the mixture has frozen, return the contents to the food processor, mix once more and return to a shallow metal pan. Place the pan in the freezer until frozen.

Banana-Pecan Ice Cream
—Toni Lydecker, food journalist and author of *Seafood alla Siciliana: Recipes and Stories from a Living Tradition* (New York, 2009)

Like a Sicilian gelato, this ice cream isn't too rich, and is thickened with cornstarch rather than eggs. Bananas also contribute to the creamy mouthfeel. In place of the pistachios typical of a Sicilian gelato, pecans from Texas were used.

½ cup (60 g) pecans
1 quart (950 ml) half-and-half (in the UK, use 475 ml single cream mixed with 475 ml skimmed milk)
¾ cup (150 g) sugar
2 tsp cornstarch
¼ tsp kosher salt
2 medium bananas, mashed well (about 1 cup)
1 tsp pure vanilla extract

Preheat the oven or toaster oven to 300°F (150°C). Spread the pecans on a baking sheet; bake until aromatic, about 5 minutes; turn off heat and cool in the oven; coarsely chop.

Combine 1 cup of the half-and-half, the sugar, cornstarch and salt in a small bowl; stir until smooth. In a medium saucepan, bring the remaining half-and-half to a boil. Stir in the sweetened half-and-half. When the mixture returns to a boil, reduce the heat and simmer until lightly thickened, about 10 minutes. Off heat, stir in the vanilla extract. Chill well.

Just before making the ice cream, add the bananas to the half-and-half mixture. Following the directions for your machine, make the ice cream. Add the pecans during the last few minutes of freezing.

Gelado de Baunilha com Banana e Caril

—with the permission of David Leite, publisher of
www.leitesculinaria.com; author of *The New Portuguese Table*
(New York, 2009); 2006 and 2007 James Beard Award winner

1 medium very ripe banana
1½ to 2 tsps mild curry powder
1 pint premium vanilla ice cream, softened in the microwave for
10 to 15 seconds

In a medium bowl, mash the banana and curry powder together with a fork until almost smooth. Add the ice cream and stir to combine. The texture should be similar to soft-serve ice cream. If it's not, place the bowl in the freezer, stirring every 5 minutes to firm up.

Spoon the dessert into chilled cordial glasses and serve.

Serves 6.

Note: Avoid making this dessert too long beforehand. It tends to mute the power and flavour of the curry powder.

Eggnog Ice Cream

— from Judith Sutton, New York cookbook author/consultant and
food writer, and co-author of *Chef Mario Batali*, among others

This unusual and sophisticated ice cream would be a wonderful finish to a New Year's Eve or Christmas dinner. The rum and whiskey (you could use ¼ cup of either one, but the combination provides a more subtle flavour) gives the ice cream an intensely creamy texture. The alcohol also means that it keeps better than other homemade ice creams, so you can prepare it well ahead, and it will still be delicious.

2½ cups (560 ml) heavy (double) cream

1 cup (225 ml) milk (or half-and-half)

7 large egg yolks

1 cup (200 g) sugar

2 tablespoons bourbon

2 tablespoons dark rum

½ teaspoon vanilla extract

Scant ¾ teaspoon nutmeg

Combine the cream and milk in a large heavy saucepan and bring just to a simmer over medium heat.

Meanwhile, combine the egg yolks and sugar in a large bowl and whisk until thick and smooth. Whisking constantly, gradually add about half of the hot milk mixture to the egg yolks, then pour the mixture back into the saucepan. Cook over medium-low heat, stirring constantly with a wooden spoon, until the custard thickens slightly and coats the back of the spoon (when you run your finger down the spoon, it will leave a track), 3 to 5 minutes; do not let boil. Immediately remove the pan from the heat and strain the custard through a fine-mesh strainer into a bowl. Let cool slightly, then stir in the bourbon, rum, vanilla, and nutmeg. Let cool to room temperature, stirring occasionally, then cover and refrigerate for at least 2 hours, or overnight.

Freeze the mixture in an ice cream maker according to the manufacturer's instructions. Transfer the ice cream to an airtight container and freeze until ready to serve. (The ice cream will not freeze as hard as ice cream made without alcohol; it keeps well for at least 3 days.)

Serves 8.

Avocado Ice Cream Parfait

—with the permission of Chef Renee Marton (MA CCP), New York,
chef-instructor and food historian

1 ripe avocado (still firm, but ripe)
6 fl. oz (175 ml) organic vanilla soy milk
3 fl. oz (90 ml) dark Agave syrup
pinch salt
1 pint (600 ml) dark fruit (boysenberry, black raspberry, cassis)
sorbet – shop-bought is fine
1 tablespoon toasted sesame seeds
1 ripe pineapple, peeled, cut in half (save half for another use),
cored, sliced and grilled
4 plastic moulds: can use disposable stiff plastic cups
(about 6 to 8 oz).

Blend together avocado, milk, Agave syrup and salt in food processor until smooth and creamy. Place a thin layer of toasted sesame seeds on bottom of plastic cup. Make sure the layer is flat with no holes

Spoon the avocado 'ice cream' gently onto the sesame seeds until the cup is filled slightly more than half.

Spoon softened sorbet onto the avocado ice cream until the cup is full, and smooth the top.

Wrap in plastic and freeze until firm. When ready to eat, remove from freezer 15 minutes ahead of time. Turn cups upside down after unwrapping, and place each one is a wide soup bowl. While holding the cup, make a cut with a sharp knife into the bottom of the cup, and squeeze the cup gently. This will release the moulded ice cream/sorbet without disturbing the sesame seeds.

Serve with grilled pineapple slices, or blueberry compote with toasted coconut flakes.

Serves four.

Note: the sorbet defrosts faster than the avocado 'ice cream', so once unmolded, you can let the dessert sit at room temperature for another 5 minutes, to soften the avocado 'ice cream', before serving.

Smoked Salmon Ice-cream

—with the permission of Chef John Williams, Executive Chef,
Ritz London Executive

600 g (20 fl. oz) whole milk
50 g (1 ¾ oz) caster sugar
50 g (1 ¾ oz) glucose powder
50 g (1 ¾ oz) dextrose
100 g (3 ½ oz) glycerine
400 g (14 oz) smoked salmon
5 g (1 teaspoon) salt

Bring all the ingredients to the boil for 2 min. Cool at 35°c. Add the chopped salmon. Blitz and pass through a chinois. Leave to infuse for 12 hours and churn.

Serves 8 portions.

References

1 Frank Brinkley and Dairoku Kikuchi, *A History of the Japanese People From The Earliest Times To The End Of The Meiji Era* (New York, 1915), p. 106.
2 Elizabeth David, *Harvest of the Cold Months: A Social History of Ice and Ices* (New York, 1995), p. 228.
3 Ibid., p. 227.
4 Jeri Quinzio, *Of Sugar and Snow: A History of Ice Cream Making* (Berkeley, CA, 2009), pp. ix–x.
5 Alberto Capatti and Massimo Montanari, *Italian Cuisine: A Cultural History* (New York, 2003), p. 110.
6 Gillian Riley, *The Oxford Companion to Italian Food* (Oxford, 2007), pp. 256–7.
7 Quinzio, *Of Sugar and Snow*, p. 19.
8 David, *Harvest of the Cold Months*, p. xv.
9 Riley, *The Oxford Companion to Italian Food*, pp. 258–9.
10 Quinzio, *Of Sugar and Snow*, p. 101.
11 Capatti and Montanari, *Italian Cuisine*, p. 259.
12 Ray Oldenburg, *The Great Good Place, Cafés, Coffee Shops, Bookstores, Bars, Hair Salons and Other Hangouts at the Heart of a Community* (New York, 1989), p. 112.
13 Jerome Charyn, *Bronx Boy: A Memoir* (New York, 2002), p. 32.

Select Bibliography

Alexander, Eleanor M. A., *A Uniquely American Watering Hole:
The Drug Store Soda Fountain At The Turn Of The Twentieth
Century (Apothecary)*, University of Delaware (Winterthur
Program dissertation, 1986)

Ashmole, Elias, *The Institution, Laws and Ceremonies of the Most
Noble Order of the Garter Collected and Digested into One Body*
(London, 1672)

Buzzell Arthur L., ed., *The Bulletin of Pharmacy*, vol. XXXVI
(Detroit, MI, 1922)

Charyn, Ray, *Bronx Boy: A Memoir* (New York, 2020)

Briggs, Richard, *The new art of cookery, according to the present practice; being a complete guide to all housekeepers, on a plan entirely new;
consisting of thirty-eight chapters . . . ,* (Philadelphia, PA, 1792)

Brinkley, Frank, *A History of the Japanese People from the Earliest
Times to the End of the Meiji Era* (Cambridge, MA, 1915)

Capatti, Alberto, and Massimo Montanari, *Italian Cuisine:
A Cultural History* (Irvington, NJ, 2003)

Clarke, Chris, *The Science of Ice Cream* (Cambridge, 2004)

Datamonitor industry profile, Ice Cream in . . . Europe, France,
United Kingdom et al. (New York, 2008)

DeRenzo, Nicholas, 'The Scoop on Savory', undergraduate
paper, New York University, 2008

David, Elizabeth, *Harvest of the Cold Months* (New York, 1995)

Day, Ivan, 'The Art of the Confectionery', at www.historic-
food.com/Georgian%20Ices.htm

Dickson, Paul, *The Great American Ice Cream Book* (New York, 1972)

Eales, Mrs Mary, *Mrs Mary Eales's Receipts* (London, 1733)

Ebert, Albert Ethelbert and Hiss, A. Emil, *The Standard Formulary* (Chicago, IL, 1904)

An Electronic History of J. Lyons & Co. and some of its 700 subsidiaries, at www.kzwp.com/lyons/index.htm

Euromonitor International, Country Sector Briefings, Ice Cream-Japan, Ice Cream-Hong Kong/China et al.

Farmer, Fanny Merritt, *The Boston Cooking School Cookbook* (Boston, 1896) online at ttp://digital.lib.msu.edu/projects/cookbooks/html/books/book_48.cf

—, *Food and Cookery for the Sick and Convalescent* (Boston, 1904), online at http://digital.lib.msu.edu/projects/cookbooks/html/books/book_56.cfm.

Fisk, Walter Warner, *The Book of Ice-cream* (New York, 1919)

Foerster, Robert Franz, *The Italian Emigration of Our Times* (Cambridge, MA, 1919)

Funderburg, Anne Cooper, *Chocolate, Strawberry, and Vanilla: A History of American Ice Cream* (Bowling Green, OH, 1995)

Glasse, Hannah, *The Art Of Cookery, Made Plain And Easy* (London, 1755)

Hansen, Eric, 'Orchid Ice Cream: An Aficionado Journeys To Turkey To Discover The Birthplace Of This Aphrodisiac Treat,' at www.salon.com/wlust/feature/1998/11/17feature.html

Hills, L. Rust, 'How To Eat An Ice Cream Cone', *New Yorker*, 24 August 1968

Hiss, Emil, *The Standard Manual of Soda and Other Beverages* (Chicago, IL, 1897)

Hopkins, Albert Allis, *The Scientific American Cyclopedia Of Formulas* (New York, 1910)

Ice and Refrigeration, XVI/1–6 (Chicago, IL and New York, 1899)

Jefferson, Thomas, vanilla ice cream recipe, Jefferson Papers, Library of Congress and at www.monticello.org/jefferson/dayinlife/dining/at.html

Johnson, Nancy M., US Patent No. 3,294 to N. M. Johnson,

'Artificial Freezer', patented 9 September 1843

Krasner-Khait, Barbara, 'The Impact of Refrigeration', *History* (February/March 2002)

A Lady of Philadelphia, *Seventy-five Receipts for Pastry, Cakes, and Sweetmeat* (Boston, MA, 1828)

Lidell, Caroline, and Robin Weir, *Ices* (London, 1995)

Lucas, P. S., 'Ice Cream Manufacture', *Journal of Dairy Science*, XXXIX/6, 833–7 (1956)

Marshall, Robert T., H. Douglas Goff and Richard W. Hartel, *Ice Cream*, 6th edn (New York, 2003)

Masters, Thomas, *The Ice Book* (London, 1844)

Meyer Druggist, XXII (St Louis, MI, 1901)

New York Times archives online (1851–present)

Nutt, Frederick, *The Complete Confectioner*, 2nd edn (London, 1790)

Oldenburg, Ray, *The Great Good Place* (New York, 1989)

Pompa, A., 'Soda Fountains in England', *Soda Fountain* (February, 1922)

Quinzio, Jeri, 'Asparagus Ice Cream, Anyone?' *Gastronomica*, II/2 (2002)

—, *Of Sugar and Snow: A History of Ice Cream Making* (Berkeley and Los Angeles, CA, 2009)

Ranhofer, Charles, *The Epicurean* (New York, 1894)

Riley, Gillian, *Italian Food* (Oxford and New York, 2009)

Sigerist, Henry Ernest, *Socialized Medicine in the Soviet Union* (London, 1937)

Websites and Associations

Trade Associations

Dairy Industry Association of Australia
www.diaa.asn.au

Dairy Association of China
www.dac.com.cn

European Ice Cream Association (Euroglaces)
www.euroglaces.eu/en

Ice Cream Alliance (Great Britain)
www.ice-cream.org

International Association of Ice Cream Manufacturers
www.iaicdv.org

International Association of Ice Cream Vendors
www.iaicv.org

International Dairy Foods Association
www.idfa.org

Japanese Ice Cream Association
www.icecream.or.jp

National Confederation of Ice Cream Producers (France)
www.lemondedudessert.tm.fr

National Ice Cream Retailers Association
www.nicra.org

New Zealand Ice Cream Manufacturers' Association
www.nzicecream.org.nz/industryfacts.htm

Manufacturers and Fan Sites

Baskin Robbins
www.baskinrobbins.com

Ben & Jerry's Homemade Ice Cream
www.benjerry.com

Good Humor
www.icecreamusa.com/good_humor

Hojoland
www.hojoland.com

Ice Screamers
www.icescreamers.com

Häagen Dazs
www.haagen-dazs.com

J. Lyons & Co.
www.kzwp.com/lyons/icecream.htm

Mövenpick
www.moevenpick-icecream.com

Nestle SA
www.nestle.com

Unilever
www.unilever.com

Wall's
www.walls.co.uk

Acknowledgements

I have many people to thank for their help with this book. I'd like to thank the New York University Arthur L. Carter Journalism Institute, particularly Chair Prof. Brooke Kroeger, Prof. Charles Seife, Pamela Noel, Prof. Mary Quigley, Rose Sculley and Kate Panuska, for their support and encouragement. Also, I'd like to thank the following chefs and food writers for their generosity in contributing recipes for *Ice Cream*: Claudia Fleming, David Lebovitz, Yumiko Kano, Pichet Ong, David Leite, Toni Lydecker, Renee Marton, Judith Sutton and John Williams. Also, I would like to thank Alex Gonzales of Havana, Cuba; Nicholas E. DeRenzo, NYU journalism student; Susan Bokern; Liz Brenna, PR Coordinator, Ben & Jerry's; David Burrows, Brand Development Director, Unilever; Dean A. Peters, Associate Vice President of Communications, American Dairy Queen Corporation; Yukari Sakamoto; Silvestro Silvestori; John T. Edge, Dana Jacobi, cookbook author; Anne Coglianese and her father, Theodore Stanley Krzywinski (Kay); Anthony Edmund Forte; Melanie Perez of Euromonitor International; Lynn Oliver, culinary librarian; Rebecca Werner of Werner Public Relations, Inc.; Yona Levy of Screme gelato; Silvestro Silvestri; Ali Choudry of the Magic Fountain in Mattiuck, Long Island; and Charles Salzberg.

A special thanks to my mother, Dorothy Simonds; my father, Edmund Simonds, and to my mother-in-law, Mili Dunn Weiss.

I couldn't have written this book without the office space provided by Waldner's Business Environments. Without the good cheer of the Waldner's staff – not to mention a steady supply of bagels and coffee – this book would never have been completed. A very special thanks to Stephen Waldner, chairman; Meredith Waldner, President; and Jay Waldner, Principal.

I'd also like to thank my agent, Alice Martel, for her guidance and suggestions. I also owe a special debt of gratitude to Michael Leaman, publisher of Reaktion books, to Martha Jay, editor of the Edible Series, for her good humour and endless patience, and to Andrew F. Smith, Series Editor. Most of all, I'd like to thank my husband, Randy Weiss, for his support and love – and for taking on the arduous task of serving as chief ice cream taster – during the writing of *Ice Cream*.

Photo Acknowledgements

The author and publishers wish to express their thanks to the below sources of illustrative material and/or permission to reproduce it. Some locations of artworks are also given below.

Photo © adlifemarketing/2010 iStock International Inc.: p. 68; photo Sabah Arar/Rex Features: p. 9; photo Jack E. Boucher: p. 52; photo A. Bruni/Alinari/Rex Features: p. 50; photo C.WisHisSoc/ Everett/Rex Features: p. 60 (foot); photos Paul Cooper/Rex Features: pp. 97, 137; photo courtesy Dairy Queen: p. 101; The Detroit Institute of Arts: p. 22; photo © dlerick/2010 iStock International Inc.: p. 65; photo John Ferrell: p. 87; photos William G. Hallbauer, from the Estate of Ernest & Bertha Hanlon, of Nahant, MA, USA, submitted by Ronald E. and Donna Lee Hanlon: p. 104; photo Hulton Archive/Getty Images: p. 67; photo Image Source/ Rex Features: p. 136; photo William Gus Johnson: p. 46 (top); photo B. W. Kilburn: p. 125; photos Michael Leaman/Reaktion Books: pp. 72, 108, 120; photo Russell Lee: p. 60 (top); Library of Congress, Washington, DC (Prints and Photographs Division): pp. 29, 46, 52, 57, 60 (top), 62, 87, 91, 117, 125; from *Lippincott's Magazine*, August 1877: p. 34; Musée National Picasso, Paris (© Succession Pablo Picasso, Paris/DACS): p. 73; National Library of Medicine, Bethesda, MD (Images from the History of Medicine Collection): pp. 24, 133; photo courtesy Archives Center, National Museum of American History (Smithsonian Institution), Washington, DC: p. 84; photo courtesy Rex Features: p. 55; photos

Roger-Viollet/Rex Features: pp. 18, 23, 28, 118; Arthur and Elizabeth Schlesinger Library on the History of Women in America (Radcliffe Institute for Advanced Study, Harvard University): p. 56; photo Alex Segre/Rex Features: p. 121; photo Sipa Press/Rex Features: p. 131; photo SNAP/Rex Features: p. 69; photo Richard Sowersby/Rex Features: p. 100; photo Ray Tang/Rex Features: p. 116; photo © Tanya_F/2010 iStock International Inc.: p. 129; photo Sue Toth: p. 115; photo Laura B. Weiss: p. 128; photo Woman's Weekly/Rex Features: p. 66.

Index

italic numbers refer to illustrations; **bold** to recipes